on their own feet

ORDERS
tel: +44 (0)20 7431 1075; fax: +44 (0)20 7435 9076
email: shop@karnacbooks.com
www.karnacbooks.com

standing on their own feet

you and your younger adolescent

Judith Trowell

You and Your Child Series
Editor, Dr A. H. Brafman

KARNAC

First published in 2008 by
Karnac Books Ltd.
118 Finchley Road,
London NW3 5HT

British Library Cataloguing in Publication Data

A C.I.P. for this book is available from the British Library

ISBN: 978-1-85575-531-4

10 9 8 7 6 5 4 3 2 1

Edited, designed, and produced by Communication Crafts

Printed in Great Britain

www.karnacbooks.com

contents

about the author

Judith Trowell is an Honorary Consultant Psychiatrist, Tavistock Clinic, and Professor of Child Mental Health, West Midlands NIMHE/CSIP and University of Worcester. She is a psychoanalyst and child analyst and worked for many years in the NHS as a clinician, trainer, and clinical researcher.

acknowledgements

My thanks to Abe Brafman for his help, support, and encouragement; to Gillian Miles for encouraging me not to give up; and to my children Stephen and Vanessa, and grandchildren Alexander, Susannah, and Henry, and Maria and Daniel, from whom I have learnt so much. But above all to my patients, who have helped me to understand them and myself.

series editor's foreword
DR A. H. BRAFMAN

Once upon a time parents celebrated the arrival of puberty with pride, and in many cultures family and community joined together to celebrate this passage from childhood to adulthood and independence. It is sad that today we live in times when this transition is viewed with anxiety and fear. Of course, as ever before, the ex-child comes to this point in his/her life with a mixture of excitement and ambivalent anticipation, but now their parents often experience a sense of isolation and dread, not knowing how to ensure that the next ten to twelve years run smoothly for their child and for themselves.

Judith Trowell has had a rich professional life working in a variety of settings and contexts with adolescents and their parents. In this book, she describes and discusses in a lucid and sensitive manner the physical and emotional changes that younger adolescents, aged between 10 and 14 years, go through and how these affect and are influenced by their parents. She also presents clinical examples that illustrate some of the problems found in early adolescence and how these can be helped.

There is a central philosophy uniting all the volumes in the You and Your Child Series. Each of the authors featured has published papers and books for the academic and clinical communities; the present volumes, however, are specifically aimed at parents. The intent is not to convince but to inform the reader. Rather than offering solutions, we are describing, explaining, and discussing the problems that parents meet while bringing up their children, from infancy through to adulthood.

We envisage that two groups of parents may choose to read these books: some may wish to find here answers to specific questions or to problems they are facing in their lives, whereas others may read them only to broaden their knowledge of human development. Our intention is that the writing should be phrased in a way that might satisfy both groups. There is an attempt at something of a translation of what children of different ages experience in their lives with parents, family, and the wider world. Our authors have based their texts on their extensive work with children, adolescents, and their parents—not only in the authors' private consulting-rooms, but also in schools, community agencies, and teaching hospitals—and, in most cases, with children of their own.

The authors aim to depict the child's experiential view of his life, helping parents to understand behaviours, thoughts, and feelings that the child may not have been able to verbalize. There is no question of being the child's advocate—no purpose is seen in trying to find who is to blame for the problems under discussion. These are, rather, interested and knowledgeable professionals attempting to get child and parents to understand each other's point of view. In our books, the authors describe in detail the increasing range of each child's developing abilities on the path from infancy to adulthood: it is this knowledge of potential and actual abilities that is fundamental for an understanding of a child's behaviour.

Many, if not most, of the books available on child development adopt the view that a child is the product of the environment in which he is brought up. To some extent, this is obviously true: the child will speak his parents' language and adopt the customs that characterize the culture in which the family live. The commonly heard remark that a particular child "takes after" a parent or other close relation bears out the fact that each growing individual responds and adapts to the milieu in which he lives—and not only in childhood, but throughout his life. Nevertheless, it is still true that not all children brought up in one particular home will show the same characteristics. From a scientific point of view, there are endless discussions on the issue of nature versus nurture. However, from a pragmatic point of view, it is certainly more correct and more useful to consider family problems with children as being the result of an interaction—who started this, and when and how it started, is virtually impossible to establish. Through their words and behaviour, child and parents continually confirm each other's expectations; they keep a vicious circle going, where each of them feels totally justified in their views of themselves and of each other.

It is not rare that the parents present quite different readings of what each of them considers their child's problems to be. Needless to say, the same can be found when considering any single issue in the life of an ordinary family. The baby cries: the mother thinks he is hungry, whereas the father may feel that here is an early warning of a child who will wish to control his parents' lives. The toddler refuses some particular food: the mother resents this early sign of rebellion, whereas the father will claim that the child is actually showing that he can discriminate between pleasant and undesirable flavours. The 5-year-old demands a further hour of television watching: the mother agrees that he should share a programme she happens to enjoy, whereas the father explodes at the pointlessness of trying to instil a sense of discipline in the house. By the time the child has reached puberty or adolescence, these clashes are a matter of daily routine. . . . From a practical point of view, it is important to recognize that there is no question of ascertaining which parent is right or which one is wrong: within their personal frames of reference, they are both right.

The problem with such disagreements is that, whatever happens, the child will always be agreeing with one of them and opposing the other.

There is no doubt that each parent forms an individual interpretation of the child's behaviour in line with his or her own upbringing and personality, view of him/herself in the world, and past and present experiences, some of them conscious and most of them unconscious. But—what about the child in question? It is not part of ordinary family life that a child should be asked for *his* explanation of the behaviour that has led to the situation where the parents disagree on its interpretation. Unfortunately, if asked, the adolescent may well fail to find the words to explain himself or may at times be driven to say what he believes the parent wants to hear; at other times, his response may sound too illogical to be believed. The myth has somehow grown that in such circumstances only a professional will have the capacity to fathom out the child's "real" motives and intentions.

It is an obvious fact that each family will have its own style of approaching its child. It is simply unavoidable that each individual child will have his development influenced—not *determined* but *affected*—by the responses his behaviour brings out in his parents. It is, however, quite difficult for parents to appreciate the precise developmental abilities achieved by their child. No child can operate, cope with life, or respond to stimuli beyond his particular abilities at any particular point in time. And this is *the* point addressed in the present series of books. We try to provide portraits of the various stages in the child's cognitive, intellectual, and emotional development and how these unfolding stages affect not only the child's experience of himself, but also how he perceives and relates to the world in which he lives. Our hope is that establishing this context will help the parents who read these books to see their child from a different perspective.

standing
on their own feet

From childhood to adolescence

Young children are cute and delightful—or they are having temper tantrums. Primary school children are eager and enthusiastic, gaining mastery of their world, defiant and difficult at times but still mainly wanting to please, responding to suggestions and requirements. Then comes adolescence, and the rules of engagement change. Young adolescents aged 10 to 14 years are still legally children, and parents/carers are responsible for them and their behaviour. However, these young people begin to see themselves as separate, independent individuals. Friendships become more intense, and the peer group becomes increasingly significant. External issues can be vital: clothes, hairstyle, make-up, activities, behaviour inside or outside school all come to signify to which group the young person belongs. Home and the family become less and less important.

Internally, of course, this is not true. The young person's significant relationships remain the parents/carers, siblings, extended family—grandparents, cousins, aunts and uncles— even though these must be denied most of the time as other friendships become increasingly significant. But the home and family can provide a sanctuary when outside relationships fracture and re-form. However, the family members may not appreciate their central position, as the young person argues and fights over most things. Contempt, sarcasm, and resentment at any restrictions escalate; mostly, nothing is good enough. This behaviour is, of course, a reflection of the young person's internal state—feeling inadequate, a failure, not good enough, frightened, uncertain.

Adolescent turmoil

What is unnerving for the young person and his/her family are the physical changes and also the changes in energy levels. At times the young person is full of energy, lively, restless, ready to go, to do whatever; at other times he/she feels exhausted, washed out, and very low. This lability, and the fluctuating mood that goes with it, is ordinary "adolescent turmoil", but it is hard to adjust to the fluctuations. The young person talks about feeling out of control or all over the place. However, parents/carers can feel that the young person is in charge and doing exactly what he/she wants and that they are the ones who are out of control and all over the place. Each blames the other, and they find it hard to recognize that they are mirroring each other.

Younger adolescents repeat the struggles of the preschool child: they have temper outbursts, find it hard to wait when they want something, and expect to be the centre of the universe and that the family will revolve around them. This leads to conflicts with parents and siblings, and discipline becomes a problem; the young adolescent may be a large, quite strong person who can no longer be made to behave or be reasonable. There are issues that emerged early on, but the management of anger (in particular, being assertive but not aggressive) is a huge problem for both the young person and the parents. Young people are emerging with their own identity, their own ideas. They have passionate beliefs but also have to tolerate others with different ideas that may be opposite to their own. Now that their bodies are bigger and stronger, they may be physically as powerful as their parents, and they have to manage to control their rage and fury when frustrated or when their wishes are blocked. Emotional storms are inevitable.

Intergenerational conflict seems unavoidable: young people need to kick against the standards and attitudes of the older generation, their appearance, how they live their lives. This conflict helps to define the young person, and to find his/her place in the intergenerational cycle, but it is not easy to bear. Parents can find themselves provoked—some of the comments can be very personal and hurtful. Parents may be hurt or angry, and the conflict can then escalate; verbal violence may spill over into physical violence unless the parents manage to restrain themselves. Some young people can be verbally and then physically violent to a parent, and this is very distressing. The young person needs, when calmer, to be advised that this is not acceptable; strategies must be proposed to avert rage when it becomes explosive. Other parents do not confront a difficult young person, preferring to back down, for a quiet life. Or if the rage is directed at one parent, then it is all too easy for the other parent to allow this to happen, to support and collude with the attacks and gain some satisfaction from being the "good" parent. This can, at the time, lead to emotional closeness, but in the long run it damages the parents' relationship and leads to the young person feeling lost, confused, and dismissive of both parents.

Emerging sexuality

Underlying some of this tension is the emerging sexuality. Adolescents are struggling to confirm their sexual identity, their gender, their sexual orientation. They face the questions: Do I want relationships with the same sex, the opposite sex, or both, and what age of partner do I want? Do I feel excited by individuals older than me (parental generation), the same age as me, or younger than me? So, consciously or unconsciously, the young person may have sexual feelings for mother or father, aunts or uncles, teachers, members of their peer group, older pupils in school, or younger children. While these feelings are all part of adolescence, how they are managed by the young person and his/her parents or carers is crucial. Thoughts and feelings may be intense, but the young person usually is left to struggle with them as wishes and desires. If the object of desire—a teacher or aunt or uncle, for example—reciprocates and responds to these intense emotions, then the young person is not only aroused but may be physically involved. This can lead to intense pressure and need for future such gratification; if this or a similar relationship is repeated, then it is as though the need and the person desired become fixed in the young person's mind. Many young people have intense longings and needs for a range of individuals; as long as these remain as longings, then there is the freedom to change. Once the relationship has regularly become a physical relationship, exploring other relationships may be problematic, particularly if this would mean a relationship change from male to female or vice versa.

Younger adolescents experiment initially in their minds, imagining what any sexual contact would be like; then there is physical experimentation, starting with petting and heavy petting and followed by more intimate physical contact. If the object of sexual interest is an adult with his/her own sexual issues and needs, then the relationship can escalate and become consuming so that the period of exploration is short-circuited, leading to a situation that is exciting but can increasingly become stuck. Young people need to allow themselves to find—and need to be allowed to find—the relationships that feel right for them.

Facing difference and conflicts

The young person has to accomplish the major developmental task of coming to terms with difference. While the peer group is imposing and demanding a rigid conformity and sameness, in reality the young person is faced with the complexity of difference, which he/she will attempt to deny. Male or female may be an obvious difference but at times can be hard to distinguish, and some young people present as neutral or androgynous. But there are many other differences: racial and ethnic; class, and all that goes with it; culture; views of the world; material standards; physical differences, which may be genetic but may also follow illness or disability. Religious differences may be limited to religious observances and holy days but may also involve fundamentally different views of the world, clothes, the role of women, diet; they all represent powerful allegiances. And all these impact on young people as they seek to arrive at their own identity—racial, sexual, and spiritual.

Young adolescents have two further important conflicts to face, the first being that of life and death. They still feel they have infinite time, that their whole life is before them, but death has become a possibility—pets die, grandparents die—and as they become more independent they are required to be more aware of danger. They begin to appreciate that life is fragile, that uncontrolled anger and hatred can lead to catastrophe, but also that there are external events, accidents, natural disasters that cannot always be avoided. Their parents' protection can achieve only so much.

As well as the recognition of death, that life will end, young people become aware of sanity and madness. They are aware that one can lose control during an angry outburst and that this is very frightening. Another sort of losing control can be even more scary—namely, losing one's mind, one's reason: seeing, hearing, thinking things that others do not. Becoming weird, doing strange things, is terrifying, and then one will be conspicuous, stand out, and not fit in.

* * *

All the above issues are discussed in more detail in this book— the pain and the struggle as well as the excitement, the fun, and the challenge of them for the young persons and for their parents and family.

The young person's internal world

Young people have a vast amount of knowledge to acquire in school, and they also have to develop social skills, join a peer group, form relationships, renegotiate their position in the family, and develop their own identity as a person with his/her own thoughts, feelings, intellectual capacities, and sexual, racial, and spiritual identity. The foundations for this emotional and psychic work are built on significant attachments and relationships. This is thinking about the internal world. They have taken inside their minds, into their internal world, the repeated experiences they have had with their parents, and these coalesce into the "internalized parental object" or attachment figure. The two parents (or carers) are internalized, and they have a relationship in the young person's mind in addition to their relationship in the external world.

Children have hundreds of thousands of small and large interactions with their parents. Those parents who are reasonably reliable and consistent become a "secure base" in the child's mind, and this is the bedrock of the child's later emotional development. At the same time, a representation of each parent and each significant person is formed in the child's mind, in his/her internal world. However, this internal representation—or internal object—of "mother" or "father" is not a direct replica of the external person. The internal representation is a combination of the external interactions, but it is also shaped by the child's emotional responses, thoughts, and feelings about the person. The internal parent thus differs from the external reality that is the parent. For example, if, when the young person was a small child, a parent suffered from depression and then recovered, the parent might now be calm and thoughtful. But the internal parent in the mind of the young person would still be flat and low and irritable, just as the parent had been during the time he/she was depressed. There is then a discrepancy between the parent in the young person's mind and the actual here-and-now parent. Over time and with patience on the part of the parent, the internal parent will slowly change, but the young person may continue at times to expect the earlier response that was the familiar one, rather than how the parent currently feels and reacts.

1

developmental stages

Early adolescence is a time of major developmental activity. There is a growth spurt, the young person's hands and feet enlarge, their arms and legs rapidly lengthen, their body and face shape changes; most disorientating for them, though, is that their sex hormones become active. Girls have breasts development and sexual hair and start to menstruate; boys grow body hair and become more muscular, and their sex organs enlarge and become active and, at times, feel out of control with erections and wet dreams.

These outward manifestations are paralleled by massive internal psychological and emotional developments. Young adolescents rework many of the developmental phases that they negotiated earlier, and this gives them the opportunity to strengthen good steps or achieve a healthier outcome where previously there were problems. In considering adolescent development, therefore, we need to review earlier stages of development.

Early developmental tasks

There has been an explosion of research in the last twenty years in the fields of infant mental health and developmental psychology. This has all indicated that babies come into the world alert, responsive, wanting to interact, and much more aware than previously recognized. They are not blobs to be shaped and moulded like lumps of clay. Babies play an active part in the process and have a profound effect on their carers. Their personality characteristics, their patterns of behaviour, and their emotional states are innate but are also fluid and capable of being changed, enhanced, or reduced, depending on the emotional environment. Intelligence or cognitive capacity is also fluid, again subject to influences from the environment.

Infants come into the world capable of the very powerful emotions of love and hate. They want and need closeness, concern, affection, and intimacy but are also capable of rage, fury, and the wish to destroy. There is a view that the negative feelings only arise as a response to the frustrations of life, but the ferocity with which some babies respond to brief or small frustrations and their prolonged refusal to be calmed or mollified seem to support the innate origins of hate. This recognition of the very early origins of love and hate (innate or developing in the early weeks after birth) is vital in our understanding of children. Children are innocent, but innocence does not involve being made of milk and honey. Rage and destructiveness are part of our humanity and, as such, need to be accepted as normal.

How carers manage negative feelings in the child and demonstrate their own capacity to manage their own rage and destructiveness is crucial. Parents find themselves very distressed at times by the strength of their feelings of anger, rage, and resentment towards their child; it can be very frightening to realize that this small person provokes such fury. When the child is being difficult and defiant or when parents are under pressure, these strong feelings can erupt. Then the parents have to bear being hated by the child, which can be very upsetting, and also bear the fact that at that moment they also hate the child. But it is the parents' responsibility to keep control of their own rage and hatred and also accept that the child hates them. The wish to retaliate, to hit out if the child has hit, kicked, or spat, is so powerful, but the parents need to protect themselves and the child so that no harm is done. Then, when the situation is calmer, they must reassure the child that he/she is still loved although some behaviours are not acceptable. Babies and small children normally oscillate between love and hate—their longing for closeness alongside their wish to destroy—and at times this leaves them fearful of both their own rage and that of others. Babies also, from the start, have sexual feelings: they are aware that parts of their bodies are more pleasurable than others and are aware of and interested in the bodies of others. It is important also to remember that babies and small children may see others as made up of part objects—that is, the face, the hands, the body—and that at times for them these may not be all part of the same person. This is a normal developmental phase, and fairly rapidly the toddler recognizes that the eyes, hands, and face belong to one person, usually a parent. We now know that babies recognize faces—the configuration of features—almost from birth, so these are not broken down into parts.

Babies and small children also feel omnipotent: they see themselves as the centre of the universe and in control, able to determine what happens. This belief that they are the centre of the universe is, though, challenged by the ordinary everyday frustrations of life—the child has to wait for tea or a favourite TV programme or has to share with a brother or sister or a little friend the whole bag of sweets or crisps when he/she wanted all of it. There will, however, also be major challenges to this omnipotence, leaving them devastated, often shattered, in pieces, and when bad things happen—a death, a divorce, a parent leaving—they believe it was their fault, their responsibility. Small children then are often deeply troubled by guilt, and telling them that it is not their fault provides little relief. How the baby or small child manages all these powerful feelings depends very much on the carers (the emotional facilitating environment). This is because small children respond much more to the emotional responses of those around them than to the verbal responses. If the adults, the parents or carers, can manage their own feelings and can be thoughtful and in touch, then even if they are sad or angry, the child is aware that they are managing the situation and are responsible. The child is then free to have his/her own feelings but not be burdened by feeling it is all his/her fault. The adults are able to sort things out as best they can, while not denying their distress or anger. A depressed parent, a stressed single parent, a difficult delivery, an unwanted baby, or a sick baby can all make this early period more demanding and problematic than usual, and it is never easy—rewarding, but not easy!

Around the age of 6 months (4 to 8 months), there is a definite developmental step. The infant becomes much more aware of others, a time called psychological birth. The infant develops attachments to whole people, and with this comes separation anxiety and stranger anxiety. Stranger anxiety is not usually understood; a stranger is someone who is not usually in the child's immediate circle. So at this time the extended family—grandparents, cousins, and family friends—appear "strangers" to the young child, and he/she responds by becoming anxious and unsettled for a while.

Also, the infant usually finds a special object—a blanket or teddy (a transitional object)—that provides emotional security and support. The infant has begun the process of individuation: a core self can now emerge that can sense "this is me and I have my own thoughts and feelings and you have your own thoughts and feelings and I want to communicate with you". From now on, intellectual development, speech, and play really accelerate. There is the development of curiosity, empathy, the wish to please, and the wish to control; but there are also temper tantrums and negativity, fears at night of abandonment. And, all too easily, these can become linked to physical developments—to feeding or to bowel and bladder control.

Bladder and then bowel control by the child are important steps for the adults too. Parents are relieved that no longer do they need to clean their child's smelly bottom and dispose of the contents of the nappy. If potty training is going smoothly, the child is more or less ready and during the day will be aware both that others use the lavatory or potty and also that it is uncomfortable and difficult to wear a bulky nappy. The child is pleased and proud to be able to perform in the "right" place, and this is a gift the child gives a loved parent (sometimes literally presenting the potty with its contents as an offering). Children at this stage feel that the bowel or bladder and their contents are part of themselves, their body/self, hence they are giving of themselves.

If children are angry or upset, they may lose control and mess or wet themselves. A parent who is stressed and angry may find this very difficult and believe the child is retaliating, angry at being told off. If a parent finds the whole business of nappies difficult, they might try to speed up the process of potty training. The parent presents the potty or takes the young child to the toilet and can become frustrated and angry if there is no result, and then a little later the child is wet or messy. The risk is that the parent becomes even more desperate to train the child and sees accidents as deliberate.

Most children are clean and dry by the time they start school at 5 years. But some continue to wet themselves at night until they are 8 or 10 years old. Most children round about 2 years of age start to be aware and want to both imitate older children or adults and go to the lavatory/potty. They also want to get out of uncomfortable wet nappies as they start to be able to walk about confidently. Some parents may try to begin training to use the potty when the child is 6 to 9 months, but even at a year or 2 years or, more rarely, 3 years the child may not be able to exercise control. All children vary as to when they can begin to achieve control. However, sometimes they can also be uncooperative or preoccupied and may not set out to please the parent. There may be a new younger sibling and the child is angry and upset and also does not want to be clean, seeing the new baby receiving all the attention while they want attention themselves.

Sexual feelings for both male and female carers are very powerful in boys and girls. By the age of 2 years, boys and girls are aware of gender differences, but it is more wanting what they haven't got—a place to grow babies, or a willy/penis. This means they are aware of what they have and what they do not have, and in their imagination they have fantasies of making babies with father or making babies with mother—that is, boys and girls have both fantasies. (They also have fantasies they can do it all by themselves—be hermaphroditic.) Young children are also quite confused about the body openings and what goes in and out of all of them. This is particularly so in relation to where babies come from, how they get out and enter the world. Children talk of babies being born from the mouth, the anus, the wee-wee hole, or the navel, and a few suggest the ears (the top of the head is the place in mythology). All these are normal confusions, and slowly the child sorts out the purpose of the different openings and the normal processes, including the possibility of Caesarean section.

Pre-school tasks

From about the age of 3 years, children have a sense of self and of their gender, their race, their place in the family. The major conceptual tasks are in place: male/female, grown up/child, and the cycle of life and death—in plants, animals, flies, even if not humans.

These children's thinking is intense. It is concrete, magical, and animistic, and they have their own sense of time. By concrete thinking is meant the way children take objects or statements at face value. A brick is a brick: it does not become a tower or a bridge or a fort—that is, symbolize something else. And with words a statement is taken literally straight, so that pretend or imagination has no meaning: "this toy train is yours" means it is settled outright and sharing or changing around is not acceptable.

Magical thinking is rather the opposite, which is confusing for the children and those around. Children who long for something or someone come to believe they can make it happen if they think hard enough. Confusions happen as parents anticipate a child's wishes, and so then the child believes he/she made it happen; then next time when it doesn't, there is great distress.

Animistic thinking is interesting. Everything possesses the life force. Trees and plants of course, but also inanimate objects: stones, tables, chairs, doors—they all have a life of their own. So the small child who falls over and hits his/her head on the corner of the table believes that the table "chose" to get in the way and trip him/her up. Everything is alive.

Communicating with these pre-school children is delightful but requires recognition of these different thought processes. These processes mean that conversations take interesting turns as this allows the children to talk and recount their view of the world and what is happening out in the park as they scrunch through the leaves and the conkers fall or are on the ground. The whole process has additional levels of meaning. "Does it hurt the leaves to jump on them? Do they like blowing in the wind?" "That big conker knew I wanted it to fall down for me. I made the wind blow to bring them down." To be followed by: "The leaves are pretty—can we stick them back on again?"

The interaction between the child and those around is vital and determines development in language, play, and social skills. Play—with its educative, fantasy, creative and motor skills aspects—opens up a wonderful arena for the child. But the key emotional relationships remain pivotal. The intensity of the love, the joy, the excitement, the hope, the fear, the rage, the envy, the rivalry, the shame, the despair, all focus on a few primary and secondary attachment figures. As part of this kaleidoscope of feelings there remain strong sexual feelings for both father and mother in boys and girls. They have to try to clarify how babies are made: if mother is pregnant then they are aware mummy has a baby in her tummy and that is where they came from, but the role of father is less clear.

The child is also, from about 3 years, able to remember emotional relationships (emotional object constancy). Piaget dated *object* constancy from about age 18 months—the toy that can be seen and is then hidden under the cushion continues to exist. *Emotional* object constancy is an emotional holding in mind: "I remember and think about my mum when she isn't there, and she is remembering and thinking about me and will come and collect me." In other words, the child can now cope with the parent's physical absence. This is important as the circle of relationships for the child enlarges, so that grandparents and close family friends remain in the mind as well as parents and siblings.

Pre-school children are also likely to slowly become aware of a whole range of situations in which other children live and grow up. Because pre-school children are sociable now, they want and need other children they can play with rather than alongside, and they can share and play cooperatively. Language is increasingly important, and so the children experience a whole range of people, situations, and attitudes.

Their awareness of disability will depend on their experience: if not disabled themselves, or if there is no one disabled within their family network, it may be that their first contact with disability occurs in this period, and how significant adults respond profoundly influences the child. When these children meet another child who is deaf or blind, they are puzzled by the lack of response—a toy held out but not taken, a smile of welcome not responded to, a question apparently ignored. Their inclination is usually to walk away and play with others. However, if the adult can talk to the blind and the sighted children and can explain about deaf and hearing children, ways can be suggested for how they can play together: the blind child can have his/her hand held and be talked through activities and can feel play material; the deaf child can be talked to and given materials to feel and look at and will respond to anything in his/her visual field.

Children with mobility problems need help, and the able-bodied children can take turns to support, push wheelchairs, and generally help. Diabetics, asthmatics and cystic fibrosis sufferers can be supported by the other children, who rapidly learn what is happening to their friends.

Normal able-bodied children may have more problems understanding neurological and mental health problems. Children with hemiplegia or paraplegia may need crutches or wheelchairs and other children may respond by assisting them, but epileptic children and children with ADHD, Asperger's syndrome, or autism can be difficult for the other children and their parents to accept, as they may cause disruptions and frightening incidents at school. If the adults feel confident and competent that they can manage most problems, then the other children sense that there are differences but that it is possible to take a matter-of-fact approach, so they can get to know the person of whom the disability is only a part. Where the behaviour is awkward and unpredictable, the adults may become anxious and feel out of their depth, and the children withdraw. Work particularly needs to be done to assist the adults, and they in turn can then help the children find ways of relating to this group of children.

Primary school years

With the start of school, the child is hopefully ready to move forward in a new way. There is the massive advance in acquiring skills—reading, writing, and maths, riding a bike, climbing—and there is pleasure and pride in these achievements. Other individuals, such as the teacher, become intensely important "best friends"; the love, hate, and sexual longings begin to be less focused on the primary carers. But it is important to remember that the feelings themselves are no less intense. These children become increasingly autonomous and also slowly relinquish their omnipotence, recognizing that they are not the centre of the Universe. The new feelings of smallness and vulnerability are painful, but there is also a reduction in the sense of responsibility and hence feelings of guilt for wrong things—although adults can all too easily revive this. The children's capacity to think and understand is still focused on what can be seen, or heard, or touched, or tasted. But they no longer think that if they have a thought then it has or will happen (magical thinking), they realize they cannot be in two places at once, for example. They also lose animistic thinking: the table they trip over and bang their shin on did not deliberately get in their way—it was their fault for not looking where they were going.

A sense of time has begun—the days of the week as school days, and weekend days, and the seasons of the year as well as day and night. But actually telling the time—the hours, minutes, and seconds—is a big task, although digital watches help. The big hand and little hand and the recognition of numbers all enable the child to master telling the time, but it is never easy.

It used to be thought that from around age 5 years there was "infantile amnesia"—that is, that early experiences were lost from memory. Many individuals cannot recall much of their early childhood, and memory before 2½ to 3 years is uncommon. Now, however, it is recognized that feelings and sensations may be recalled but that these early preverbal experiences cannot be, and have not been, stored and coded as memories that depend on verbal or symbolic representation. It is likely that once at school, the mind is learning and developing, so symbolic material can be stored in memory for retrieval, which can then easily be recalled. Early learning is much more body-focused, on sensations and feelings, and is linked to relationships, so that retrieval consists of powerful feelings linked to tiny fragments or incidents. Early memories certainly are there and are important, but they often emerge indirectly—that is, when triggered off by some event or thought.

Primary school children have intense feelings, but these feelings are diverted: riding bikes or horses, playing vigorous games, telling rude jokes, and generally fooling around. At the same time, having clarified earlier on whether they are male or female, boy or girl, they have to establish emotionally and in their mind which gender they are so as to feel comfortable in their body. Most boys enjoy physical activities—football, running, jumping, climbing. They are learning to be active and to get on with doing things such as swimming, trampolining, riding their bikes. What they wear tends to fit with this lifestyle: easy comfort, but with an eye to what others are wearing—fashion consciousness is around. Some boys do enjoy other physical activities: they may want to draw, play with a chemistry set, model trains, Meccano, or complex Lego. Others enjoy learning a musical instrument. These areas of play are more unisex, enjoyed by boys and girls. They involve feelings and talents such as artistic or musicality or skills in hand–eye coordination and manual dexterity. Pretend play is seen as more for girls—shops, dolls' houses, dressing up. The girls may wear either trousers or skirts, but they are very aware of what is "in fashion".

All children seem to watch television, DVDs, and videos, have Gameboys, and use the computer. It does seem that even at this age peer pressure to wear fashionable items of clothing and footwear is powerful, so that parents may have to relinquish their ideas of what is appropriate. Keeping girls as children and not allowing precocious sexuality to intrude is not easy. There is also a slow exploration by the children, thinking about, first, their sexual orientation, their ideas about heterosexuality, bisexuality, or homosexuality; then, second, when that choice of possible partner has been considered, further considerations of the object choice. If a girl has moved to a heterosexual orientation, she has to decide whether she will then have a male partner who is much older—her parents' generation—or her own age or younger. These thoughts are only just beginning to emerge in primary school children, focused mainly around celebrities and TV programmes.

Primary school children should have the emotional and mental space and time to explore these issues before actual sexual activity begins. They may find it very hard to put these thoughts and feelings into words, and, as with younger children, play and drawing may be an easier way to communicate. But they may also use the third person or a story or a fantasy. Computers and games can be used to distance and defuse the issues but also to communicate in safety.

Adolescence

With the onset of puberty and the transfer to secondary school, the equilibrium achieved is broken up. This emotional maelstrom is provoked by the growth spurt and the explosion of hormones, with the imminence of adulthood and the approach of genital sexual encounters that might lead to procreation.

If a child is struggling with or curious about relationships, then talking about the characters in their games or in their drawings and who they like and do not like, and why, can open up the issue. These children often are quite shy and need time to put any questions or worries into words. They may also chat away to a school friend, and referring back to this can let them know you are interested in their ideas. Often children feel that parents are so busy that it is better to say nothing, so the main hurdle to be crossed is letting the children take their time and not wanting to rush them. It is a delicate balance, because parents often feel they try hard, they ask questions, they try to talk to the young person, but the young person gives them the brush off. This can be quite hurtful for a parent who is trying to be interested and wants to understand. At the same time, the young person can feel that his/her parents never have time for him/her, that they are busy working or out meeting friends. At this stage, parents do need to make time, and they may find themselves sitting alone with the young person up in his/her bedroom, unwilling to come down; however, at other times—and this is frequently quite late in the evening—the young person may wander in and be quite open and eager to talk. Parents then need to avoid yawning despite being very tired and really listen to the young person and how he/she feels if they are to learn what is happening for the young person. Such meetings can create considerable conflicts between the parents, and it is important to ensure that they cooperate with each other.

The intellectual spurt that occurs with the shift to abstract thought and the capacity to develop hypotheses—hypothetical thinking—is exciting and fun. There is a clarity of mind, numerous debates, a desire to change the world, but there is in addition a torment of self-doubt and emotional pain and distress as new projects or ideas are seen to be ill-founded and as new relationships lead to let-down or betrayal. The idealism oscillates with cynicism, contempt, and derision. The omnipotence of early childhood re-emerges, with a sense of being able to do it all, change it all, knowing so much better and more than those boring conventional adults and having much more in common with their friends and their peers. But then when the sense of omnipotence crashes, is seen to be untrue, the resultant despair leaves a depressed and withdrawn young person, who may opt for the excitement and release of substance abuse, alcohol, or adolescent criminality such as taking and driving away or gang warfare. As individual omnipotence has to be given up, it is the group that is idealized and that holds all the answers. Allegiances such as to football supporters' clubs or pop-group fan clubs are assumed with an intensity bordering on fanaticism. These allegiances do indeed have tremendous significance, because they give the individual an identity and define dress, behaviour, and use of time. What is being conveyed here is that for each individual young person, there is a move from childhood omnipotence ("I can make my wishes come true" and the subsequent "my parents are the centre of the world and know everything") to the search for his/her own independent views, ideas, and knowledge. In the first instance, this is achieved by finding an identity in their peer group as they move out of the immediate family.

An adolescent needs the group both to provide this sense of identity and then, within it, the space to experiment and explore what sort of person he/she is: "who am I, what do I really like, want to be, need?" At this time of emotional lability—when feelings swing dramatically and, at times, for no obvious reason—the young person needs the security of this external identity with "the group" to manage his/her internal bewilderment and confusion. At these times parents need to be around and available if the young person wants to talk, but they must also recognize how important this group of friends is and tolerate the lengthy phone calls or the requests for lifts in the car at inconvenient times—perhaps even manage to avoid negative comments about unusual clothes or headgear, make-up, or body decoration (even piercings or tattoos!).

Early adolescence is a time for reworking sexuality. If as a small child they were left confused or uncertain about their body gender, this may arise again. Most individuals are clear about their body gender; what is more uncertain is their mind gender—their emotional and psychological view of themselves.

For girls, the onset of menstruation is emotionally highly significant. Often the bleeding can imply to the girl that she is damaged internally, that there is something wrong with her (even if intellectually she knows about "periods"). To accept menstruation as a positive, healthy demonstration of her body's development, the girl needs to have around her a mother or older woman who enjoys her own sexuality, her own body. She needs to be given "permission" to enjoy her body by an emotionally significant woman if she is to be able to fully develop and take pride and pleasure in herself. Similarly, as boys develop and become men, they need to have confidence in their bodies. They need significant male and female carers to be appreciative of their development, their physique, their change of voice.

Most adults find boys' development easier to cope with than girls', and it seems to be a less emotionally charged issue for them. This may be because, with girls, the underlying fear is of possible pregnancy and a wish that puberty and menstruation had been delayed. It might also be because the mother, who perhaps is struggling with the menopause and her own declining sexual power, sees the young girl's transformation into a sexual young woman as a threat that is too painful to bear. Fathers, too, may be fearful: perhaps they might be attracted to the new sexual young woman in the household. They have to control their feelings as they face their own declining power and the routine nature of their long-standing marital relationship.

Once young people are clear about their bodies and their emotional and psychological sexuality, they have to rethink the kind of other they want as a sexual partner. This means they have a massive mental and emotional task to accomplish, and they need personal space and time to do this. They are likely to embark on a series of relationships of varying intensity, some with the same gender, some with the opposite gender. They may also have intense relationships with older people—teachers or sixth-formers, footballers or other celebrities. Sometimes they may spend a great deal of time with younger children, baby-sitting, helping friends and relations with their families. Some young people find it all too difficult and retreat into themselves; they may be extremely shy or isolate themselves with their computer, music centre, or TV; this is particularly so if they are afflicted with troublesome acne. Most young people have the freedom to explore the range of relationships, unless, sadly, they have become active at a very young age in a full sexual relationship and have limited their options by becoming fully involved. If a young adolescent seeks same-sex partners, these partners may be a similar age to him/her; more worryingly for parents, though, will be when the young person chooses partners who are much older or much younger than him/herself. Parents then need very carefully to find ways of talking to him/her; this choice of partner may still be part of the adolescent exploration but might also be the emergence of a firm sexual orientation. Parents may need help and support to manage this.

2

aspects of development

Cognition

A part of the development process that needs specific consideration is individuals' ideas about themselves within the context of their family and their community.

It is important to understand this as a part of how thinking develops. This is a complex process that can be blocked, damaged, or distorted by, for example, abuse or trauma. One aspect, as mentioned earlier, is the capacity for empathy: the individual recognizes the existence and importance of the other and tries to stand in his/her shoes, to appreciate how he/she might be thinking and feeling. This is constantly checked with what the other is saying and doing. The individual is interested in and concerned for the other.

Then there is the development of the emotional aspect of thinking: the awareness that difficult, painful, or intense feelings can be managed, processed, and contained—that is, converted into manageable feelings. Babies and small children realize (hopefully) that their main carer, usually the mother, is in touch with how they are feeling, understands these feelings, can cope with them and think about them, is not damaged or destroyed by them, and does not retaliate. The mother can say "I know you hate me and are very angry I have kept you waiting, but here is your feed." She may also be able to say "I feel angry and cross—I have to stop what I am doing to get your feed, but I have done it anyway because I still care about you even when you are angry with me." Slowly the babies, young infants, and older children develop this capacity for themselves, to recognize and acknowledge the difference between their own feelings and those of the other person and then to be able to think clearly about what to do.

This process is important for cognitive development because it underpins language development. This is portrayed in Figure 2.1. The small child has feelings sensations in his/her stomach that are linked with hunger. If these feelings have been felt many times and satisfied with warm breast milk, a bottle, or a biscuit, the small child has a picture an icon in his/her mind (symbolic equation) of the milk or biscuit. If mother frequently says "oh, you are hungry: do you need milk, or a biscuit?" the child learns the word, the symbol, and says "milk", or "biscuit" ("biccy"!). This fairly rapidly becomes "I want a biscuit", and language flows. Once children have learnt that they can make sounds that others understand and that they can understand others, language opens up for them. But it is focused on the world around them and what is happening (concrete thinking). By early adolescence, young persons are aware of the wider world: of school, their group of friends, their country, other parts of the world. They are

Feelings	→	Symbolic equation	→	Symbol words	→	Language
Hunger in a small child		A picture in the child's mind of warm milk or a biscuit		Mother may say, "Oh, you are hungry, are you? Here is a biscuit."		Child may say, "I am hungry. Can I have a biscuit, please."

Figure 2.1. Example of the development from feelings to language

now capable of thinking about, say, the environment or world poverty; these concepts involve them in abstractions, so they are having abstract thoughts, thinking about ideas that do not directly connect with their lives.

Hopefully, as they become older adolescents, they develop hypotheses, ideas, views about what they can do. This may be in their own lives or what needs to be done nationally or globally, whether they should become vegetarian, or go and work overseas in their gap year, or join a campaigning group. They are now thinking creatively about their lives.

The final step is the capacity to look at and consider complex issues from various perspectives, to weigh things up and try to find a balance that feels right or is the least detrimental. They can then, hopefully, think and reflect and manage the conflicts that are inevitable and make satisfactory decisions that are constructive for them and those around them.

Different children are born with different intellectual abilities and degrees of inquisitiveness, but this whole developmental process is very dependent on the emotional environment: the adults that are around them are significant. To facilitate this major mental development, parents and carers need to be able to manage their own intense positive and negative feelings and contain these and, at the same time, the intense feelings of their children.

Moral development

For small children, morality—what is right or what is wrong—is often clear-cut and definite, to do with fairness, but above all to do with being found out. Based on the omnipotence that is still central in their emotional lives, situations and events are generally seen as good, all positive, or bad, all negative; but now, looking at the moral dimension, this good/bad divide continues for much longer than the emotional divide. Small children become incensed if "it's not fair", if they see another getting away with something because grown-ups did not notice. They also have a sense of morality based on ownership: a toy is owned and given intense emotional significance, so being expected to share is an outrage—unfair, bad, unthinkable. Alongside this, there is a belief in a harsh, critical judgemental world where they will easily be blamed, condemned, found guilty. So there is often considerable anxiety if they do something they believe to be wrong, fearing that they will be found out.

Gradually, during primary school, morality changes. As the child grows, a sense of morality should hopefully become more internalized—no longer fearing being caught or found out or blamed, but an internal voice that warns the child that an impending action or thought is wrong, that it will cause pain or damage to themselves or to others. Initially, this internal voice is predominantly self-protective, wanting to keep one-self out of trouble, but gradually recognition of the rights of and responsibilities for others becomes part of a moral sense. Clearly the development of this sense of right and wrong is largely dependent on the attitude and behaviour of the parents and carers. What is said to the child is important, but children learn most from what their parents do and how they react. Parents who in their own interactions are concerned for others and who try to be as honest as possible with each other, with the children, and with those around them will then talk about the conflicts and the struggles they have. Stealing in the home or from outside, pushing and shoving others out of the way, lying to cover mistakes or cheating are examples of behaviour that children observe; how parents manage these incidents themselves are what children absorb.

In adolescence, morality becomes harsh and cruel again and young persons become very sensitive to the injustices and wrongdoings in the world, feeling responsible for them and that they must put them right. At the same time, they are very judgemental of themselves and of each other, so that the pressure to conform with the peer group, and the contempt and derision for those who do not, is intense. Many become intensely religious, finding in one of the religions a moral code that clarifies many of the uncertainties and ambiguities that confront them—sexual relationships, relationships with the parental generation, the longing for material possessions, their sense of responsibility for the planet, other people. This external moral code can be very helpful if the young person is able to internalize it and find a balance between his/her own individual and family morals and that of his/her chosen religion. Whether they remain religious depends in part on this balance but, of course, is also dependent on whether they retain a belief in God or become an atheist. Whether or not they remain religious, they will, hopefully, develop a moral code that contains respect and responsibility for themselves and others and a recognition of certain fundamental rights and wrongs as well as of whatever is enshrined in the legal system of right and wrong and justice.

Spirituality

Separate from religion, but linked to it and to creativity, is the development of a sense of spirituality, of wonder, and a capacity to be in touch with an essential part of our humanity. We have bodies, we have minds that think, we have emotions and feelings, and we also have something variably called a soul or spirit. When we respond to a sunset, a rainbow, a piece of music, or perhaps a sports person who appears effortlessly to accomplish a superb feat, we sense something larger than ourselves, outside ourselves, and we feel in awe. Spirituality is a quality that is hard to explore because trying to capture it in words feels as though it loses the magic, but it is a quality that encircles our lives. We need to encourage our young people to appreciate and enjoy something outside themselves but that touches them emotionally and intellectually too, that it is all right to feel moved. And this is important because it enables us to value our humanity and also to step outside ourselves and gain or regain a sense of perspective on the more routine aspects of life.

Understanding their bodies

As children grow and develop, they have inside them in their minds an internal representation of their body (a body ego). This is the earliest image we develop of ourselves, giving us a sense of who we are—personality and capacities come later. This internal body image is built up from all the sights and sensations we have of our own bodies, from when we were and are touched or held by others and how others look at us and also when we explore parts of our body.

The child gradually builds up this body picture, and part of this will include "I am able-bodied" or "I am disabled". This will be based on their observations of themselves and others. By their response the adults around determine for these children how other children will react and behave. The adults can influence how the child faces and reacts to others and, by their attitude and behaviour, encourage the other children to accept and value the disabled child. Children with a physical disability are acutely sensitive to the reactions of others and have already compared themselves to those around them. Children with a chronic illness that leads on to disability likewise recognize this very rapidly. Children with a sensory deprivation, where there are no external signs, such as deafness, can become confused and bewildered before their deafness is recognized, as can some partially sighted children.

These children may experience a range of difficulties with other children. Physically disabled children are easily ignored, marginalized, or excluded. Children with a sensory deprivation can seem puzzling, annoying, or difficult and may be treated harshly—perhaps punished rather than ignored. They spend enormous amounts of energy struggling to be "normal" able-bodied rather than being accepted and valued as they are and provided with the assistance they need.

Children with learning difficulties may or may not have physical difficulties in addition. Often they find other children can be cruel and excluding, calling them thick or stupid, particularly if the responsible adults do not give a clear lead. They too struggle to understand themselves and how they are different.

With all disabilities, the most frequent issue is that others are surprised, shocked, or discomforted, do not know how to respond, and, so, frequently walk away. The disabled child becomes used to this and can easily see him/herself as bad or wrong rather than different. Where children are integrated from the start and disabled children are in settings with able-bodied children, the problems are much less because the children accept each other as they are. Any disabled child needing specialist input can always have this in addition to the general provision in nursery school or in primary or secondary school. Hopefully, only a very small number of profoundly disabled children and young people need separate provision.

All children have to come to terms with their appearance, their bodies and how they function, able-bodied and disabled children together need to explore what they each need. Children very quickly learn how to communicate, how to take account of each other's limitations, and how to care for and encourage each other.

Social development

As implied throughout this chapter, babies, children and young people are innately social beings. From the start, we seek and need relationships with others. Human beings are acutely sensitive and responsive to each other. Reciprocity develops early and the capacity to share follows this.

Initially, there are intimate relationships within the family. As they grow, children want and needs the stimulation of others, of other adults and other children. The endless fascination begins of wanting to know about and understand others. "Theory of mind" explores our capacity to be aware that we each have a mind, thoughts, and feelings and that others also have minds and that throughout life we want to explore these other minds. Friendship involves mutual exploration, getting to know each other and then enjoying shared activities. Hopefully, intimate relationships grow out of these friendships, and then touching, body contact, and mutual pleasure become part of the relationship at a physical level as well as an emotional and intellectual sharing.

As well as intimate, usually paired relationships and friendships that involve a few individuals, there are social groupings. These relationships generally do not involve physical intimacy and there is limited sharing of thoughts and feelings, but the group share enough to develop a sense of values, interests, and activities that bring them together and provide a sense of belonging and of companionship. It is frequently within the context of these groupings that close friendships and intimate pairings develop.

Memory

Alongside all other areas of development and, in a sense, underpinning development is memory—the capacity to record, store, retrieve, and recall events, experiences, and knowledge. There are a number of conceptual frameworks for understanding memory and how it functions, and this is a current preoccupation with psychologists, neurophysiologists, engineers, computer scientists, psychotherapists, artists, writers, biologists, and many more.

Memory can be understood biologically as genetically determined, with storage like a system of computer files or as a psychological system influenced by emotions and the context of the experience. In reality, it is likely to be a combination of these systems if the complexity and sophistication of our minds is to be recognized. We know that a vast amount of data comes from within our bodies and from the external world through our sensory receptors and in the form of second-hand knowledge via books, radio, television, and other people, and all this is stored. The traditional distinction between short-term and long-term memory no longer explains the process we call memory, although with ageing the distinction is an important and useful concept.

In childhood, what is remembered seems linked to the emotions and the context, to the physical and emotional state of the mind. Memory has been divided into conscious, preconscious, and unconscious: conscious memory is what we can easily recall, preconscious is what we can bring back with a struggle, and unconscious is stored but unavailable for retrieval and recall. The latter—unconscious memory—can suddenly re-emerge in response to a trigger or be apparent to others because a decision or behaviour seems to be based on something more than the current situation. This links with the computer model, where files can appear to be inaccessible but, if the right trigger or key word is entered, the file/memory re-emerges. The unconscious has been further divided into the unconscious containing the forgotten (but also perhaps for emotional reasons pushed away, "forgotten" to relieve emotional pain or distress) and the deep unconscious. In the deep unconscious will be all the body memories and data and also the highly charged emotional fears, fantasies, and traumas.

A conceptual framework that is helpful here is that of implicit and explicit memory. Explicit memory is the way most things we know, learn, and experience are stored. We may, with greater or lesser ease, be able to retrieve and recall these memories—the computer file-system links again.

Implicit memory is where all the early sensory and body memories—the nonverbal emotions and sensations—are stored. It has been possible to demonstrate (Perry et al., 1995; Schore, 2001) that certain overwhelming traumatic experiences pass straight into implicit memory. They presumably cannot be thought about, cannot be symbolized, and are stored with sensations and feelings. Whether these memories emerge again, in part or totally, is currently being explored.

This is a vast subject that is enormously exciting as it brings together so many disciplines and aspects of our development— the physical, emotional, psychological, and social development of the individual, the group, and society. How do we remember, what is permissible to the individual, the family, the community, and how does society manage this complex system? When intellect and rationality were the only issues, the group and society were clear, and the rules and laws of society could be defined. Today, further understanding of the significance of the emotional context and the different forms of memory is placing uncertainty in the centre.

This further understanding is developing as a result of advances in the neurosciences and neuro-imaging, through which we are learning much more about the importance of the emotional context, the state of mind of the individual and how he/she feels, and the impact this has on thinking and memory. Where experiences are stored, how they are stored, and when and how they can be recalled or accessed—as thoughts or feelings, together or separately—all mean that we are left aware that we are on the verge of understanding much more about our mental life. We already recognize that what is an apparently objective and rational idea, thought, or action has, in fact, many emotional components and can be viewed from many perspectives differently. It is an exciting but unsettling period—staying with uncertainty is still not easy.

Conclusion

Childhood is a fascinating and puzzling period. Recognition of differences in children and young people has occurred only late in human development. How their bodies develop has been studied intensively. How their minds develop their thoughts, feelings, and personality is now on the agenda. But there is still much we do not know. The internal world of a girl, a black child, a disabled child, each must be different, each must have unique individual differences. We do not know how internal universal phantasies interact with the external realities of each individual to result in a person's experience of him/herself. All of us who have contact with young people need to keep an open mind so that we can constantly review, adjust to new ideas, and learn about childhood development—that is, continuously check whether our perceptions and assumptions truly correspond to those of the individual children themselves.

Our universal humanity means that we all have many common, shared basic experiences, feelings, and capacities. This includes the core emotions of love, hate, and sexual longings. These core emotions become the basis for internal phantasies such as the Oedipal myth of sexual relationships between parents and children, or murderous rage and the myth of Abel and Cain, or killing one's parents or child. Across cultures, religions, and ethnic groups, these actions are unacceptable and are prohibited in law, have achieved mythological status, but are also in each individual's internal world as "universal phantasies". They therefore need to be acknowledged and the feelings managed, because alongside the frustration that limits impose, there comes the growth of real and deep emotional bonds that can provide joy, support, and commitment.

the young adolescent

With the arrival of puberty, parents become anxious, fearing some catastrophe. It is a time of rapid change physically and emotionally, and psychologically the young person is in flux.

Parents fear that their daughters will become pregnant and that their sons will get involved with the "wrong set" and be led astray. The media do not help, with constant accounts of the high teenage pregnancy rate, the amount of drug use particularly in clubs, or alcohol consumption as an epidemic. Violence and the knife/gun culture is also very frightening. But most young people are not in gangs, not out on the streets every night, though they may be out and about at weekends. Young adolescents cannot legally buy alcohol or cigarettes but do, of course, have older friends and acquaintances who will buy these for them.

Sexuality

Adolescence is not an easy stage for parents to manage: they remember their own adolescence and know only too well that to forbid something is to enhance its desirability. Sex education and education about drugs and alcohol does not seem to be very effective in adolescence and perhaps should be focused on the primary-school-age children, at 9, 10, 11 years of age.

A boy of 19 reported that at primary school he had done well in the football team and also with the work. Then, at secondary school at age 12 or 13, he suddenly became very interested in sex and girls. He discovered pornography on his computer and became obsessed by this. He managed to scrape into university, just, but then dropped out in his first year when he spent all his time on his computer.

Many young adolescents such as this young man are awkward and afraid and do not have social skills to manage their intense feelings in an appropriate way. They are too embarrassed and do not know how to engage others in conversations or activities, and relationships build up slowly, sometimes leading to sexual contact. Others rush into sexual intimacy without there being a relationship, so that the person has no meaning; drugs or alcohol make this easier and more likely. Young adolescents need their peer group, their friends of the same age, but like Sue Townsend's Adrian Mole, or David Mitchell's Jason in *Black Swan Green,* mostly their sexual activities are their fantasies.

Reading and speech difficulties

For boys and girls sporting prowess is very important, and academic excellence is mocked if it becomes obvious. Perhaps the most important academic skill is literacy, the ability to read and write. If a young person has dyslexia or specific reading difficulties or speech problems, then it is important to obtain appropriate help as soon as possible. It may be that these problems arise because of emotional turmoil and stress in the family, but they can also emerge with transfer to secondary schooling, when previously there had been no obvious emotional or psychological underlying problem. If not tackled at the time, the embarrassment and distress can quite quickly lead to anger and aggression or depression and despair. Either way the young person is likely to withdraw and opt out before long, feeling that the humiliation is too much to bear.

The adolescent with such problems needs a good assessment with a psychologist or speech and language therapist and then the appropriate help, which may include some psychodynamic therapy or educational therapy. Very rarely there may be problems such as selective mutism, when he/she refuses to speak outside the home, or other mental health problems that prevent this learning.

Friendships and communicating

For girls in particular, friendships are very important. Young adolescent girls have very close, emotionally intimate friendships, but there is usually a great deal of pain and distress as "best friends" split up and connect with others, and many girls are left feeling betrayed and wounded as their "best friend" moves on. These intense relationships are very important, and they involve hours on the telephone after school and lengthy computer sessions in chat rooms. As with the boys and pornography, girls can use computers to access general chat rooms if they feel lonely and excluded; this may be helpful but can also be risky.

Both girls and boys in early adolescence need some freedom and personal space, but they do also need adults who take an interest in what they are doing and talk to them about their school activities and out-of-school activities and what they are doing on the computer. With their music and their earphones, they can all too easily cut themselves off. They can appear dismissive and disorientated and may be rude, but a parent who is available and takes an interest will from time to time be rewarded with a conversation where reconnection and understanding emerges.

A girl of 14 was struggling with her schoolwork and had been seen self-harming at school, scratching her forearms. She felt she was a nuisance and in the way at home. Father had a new partner and baby; she lived with her mother in a small flat, and mother had a new boyfriend. They were absorbed in this new relationship, and she was embarrassed but also wishing she did not exist. It emerged that the flat was open-plan and she did not have a door to her sleeping area, so she was very aware of her mother and boyfriend. A door for her room and some family work to look at her relationships with both her parents certainly helped. She still felt that the other girls at school did not like her, but slowly this improved after some individual sessions.

Self-harm, suicidal thoughts, and eating disorders

It was thought that only girls self-harm, but it is now recognized that some boys also damage themselves. Scratches or cuts on the forearms or the thighs are the usual signs, and these areas are generally covered up with long sleeves and trousers or jeans. More severe cutting can involve the abdominal wall, but this is infrequent. Young people talk about feeling hopeless, wishing they did not exist, or just dead, lifeless, inside. This may not be how they feel or appear most of the time; however, when something goes wrong at school or at home, then they retreat and these feelings surface. Most of these young people are not suicidal but are seeking release and relief from the stress and distress they feel. Cutting seems to provide this release, and the sight of blood often helps them feel alive. They need to find other ways to reduce the stress, perhaps by talking to parents, siblings, close friends, or someone outside the immediate family. If the young person is unable to stop, then professional help is needed, with psychotherapy and family work.

If a young person has suicidal thoughts and overdoses or seriously cuts him/herself or is taking serious risks, help is needed fairly rapidly to reduce the danger. This may be individual therapy or group work or family work plus safety precautions. Young adolescent boys may be more likely to engage in taking risks, carrying a knife, and as part of a gang being involved with fast cars or muggings or breaking and entering or football-supporter violence.

There may be a link between uncertainty about the right to exist and suicidal thoughts and eating disorders. Anorexia or bulimia mainly affects girls. By controlling their intake or by vomiting after filling their stomachs with fattening foods, sufferers who are obsessed by their body image manage to avoid weight gain and pursue slimness. If left unchecked these eating disorders can result in quite serious, life-threatening situations. But many girls, and some boys have a mild form, which means they are constantly aware of their shape and size. For these girls, their ideal seems to be a pre-pubescent body, with no menstruation or body hair.

It is not easy to know when "dieting" slips over into an eating disorder. Bulimia, with the secretive vomiting, is more obvious; anorexia becomes apparent if the young person gets distressed and in a panic when expected to eat a full meal or when weight has been put on. Mild eating disorders can be managed and may, to a certain extent, be part of the group culture. But when it starts to dominate the young person and family events and meal times, then help needs to be sought. Young people are adept at covering up, with baggy T-shirts and trousers, the extent of their thinness, and this may be hidden unless the parents actively check the weight and observe the food intake.

Understanding the young adolescent

All these examples of young adolescents and how they cope, or not, arise from the emotional and psychological turmoil they have to manage. The confusion and distress—of not knowing themselves, not being in control of their reactions and feelings, and their longing to kick over the traces and do things their way and yet their fear of this—are powerful.

Robert Gosling (1975) writes: "perhaps the most pervasive influence on the adolescent is the projection on to him of hopes for the future". In other words we the adults, as parents, recognize our own mistakes and our own unfulfilled wishes, hopes, and expectations, and we pass these on to the young adolescent; these unspoken visions then confuse and overwhelm the young person and his/her sense of identity. Young adolescents are somewhere between the primary school "latency" period and the more settled adult state, or, as Margot Waddell (2006) describes it, "between their infantile past and the possibility of a mature adult future". They have to give up the familiar childhood identity and place in the family and take on the unrealizable aspirations as well as the unfamiliar sexual desire and aggression that flare up inside them, while trying to cope with the sense of being misunderstood and deprived. The developmental thrust towards independence and new sorts of intimacy are another aspect that the young adolescent has to manage. The young adolescent in this fluid state of transition needs to experiment and explore to arrive at his/her sense of identity and sexual identity. It is not surprising that there are problems and difficulties, but most negotiate this period with reasonable support from parents and their peer group. The creativity and capacities of the older adolescent await them; this is the time to separate and manage their physical and emotional changes.

4

mental health concerns

Emotional health and psychological well-being form the goal for all our young people, but all too often adversity of one sort or another deflects their path. Some young people may have been born disadvantaged, with a physical disability or a genetic predisposition. In childhood, there may have been difficulties, physical illness, family tensions and problems, or social upheaval. Young people therefore enter adolescence with a range of mental health concerns, some of which they may be aware of, others not. As indicated in the chapters on development, adolescence is a time of turmoil for young people. They all become anxious and have low mood at times, they all become excited, passionate, and omnipotent, and they all have to struggle with these mood swings. They also have to manage their transition in the family, from dependent child to the young person who wants independence, believes he/she can be responsible, but then needs support and help when situations or relationships go badly wrong.

Parents, not surprisingly, find these swings difficult at times. The situation had been clearer with the young person as a child: the parents had house rules and methods of discipline, and both the parents and the child knew the limits, the boundaries of what was acceptable and what was not, in their family.

As the child becomes the young adolescent, all this has to be renegotiated. The young person wants to be independent now, and the parents are only too well aware of their responsibilities still for him or her, their wish to encourage the young person's development so he/she can begin to be responsible for him/herself, but also their need to protect him or her from making too damaging mistakes. Parents and young people inevitably get it wrong at times: parents may impose rules that are too strict, which the young people then break; or the young people are given too much freedom and can get into difficulties, perhaps with alcohol or drugs. Some of the areas of complaint and conflict are money, clothes, keeping up with school work, hair (its length, style, and colour), helping at home, and keeping their bedroom tidy, whether it is their own or shared—the young people want to be more grown up but resent the work and responsibility that go with this new status.

Adolescence is a difficult time, and each young person and his or her parents struggle with the amount of independence he or she can have and the amount still needed from parenting—that is, being told what to do or being forbidden to do things. Parents need to compromise to allow the young person the opportunity to explore and take some risks, but they remain responsible. The young people must go to school and need to be looked after practically. They need a warm, dry house, food, clean clothes, and many of the extras of modern life such as mobile phones. Compromise is what needs to be achieved, but it is not easy, and parents must retain a watching, monitoring supervisory presence. The young person is likely to have mood swings; a volatile mental state is normal, but if it becomes too excited and high, or too low and despairing, for lengthy periods, then parents should notice and be concerned.

If a parent is a single parent, perhaps following divorce or bereavement or because the young person's other parent was never involved, then adolescence is a real challenge. Instead of sharing the tasks with a partner, the parent has to be both the caring, supporting, listening parent and the firm, strong parent that can set appropriate boundaries and time limits. A single parent needs to be able to think and make realistic judgements, not lean on the young person as a substitute partner or keep him/her as a younger child to avoid facing his/her move towards independence—a very difficult challenge.

Personality and difference

Many young people rapidly become quite mature and can be thoughtful and reflective. This capacity to mentalize, to think about thinking, depends on healthy early relationships, as previously discussed, so that there are good-enough internal object relationships—that is, emotional resources in the mind based on the loving relationships they have experienced already. By this is meant that the young person develops in his/her mind the capacity to reflect and think before acting or reacting. The parent who had understood the child's feelings and was, over the years of childhood, able to put the emotions into words helped the child develop his/her own capacity to experience the feeling, think about it, and then consider his/her response. When this parental input was lacking, the young person has an impulsive reaction to a situation; thought may follow later. The capacity to contain the feelings, think, and reflect before reacting, or not reacting, is the precursor of the development of the ability for self-control. These young people slowly become able to manage themselves, their feelings, their reactions, and their behaviour, to have control over themselves.

Some young people, however, appear mature but may be pseudo-mature, having become independent and self-sufficient rapidly following relationship difficulties; others remain dependent and childlike and are slow developers or unconsciously want to remain safe and secure as a child. Sometimes these difficulties can go beyond what is appropriate, and the young person has real difficulties that he/she may or may not recognize. The young people who are fiercely independent, insisting they need no one, may then have a crisis when they are unable to cope.

A girl of 13, whose parents had separated, had lived with her mother and had then moved to live with her father. Both parents, in their different ways, tried to protect her and set reasonable limits, but she insisted that she could manage fine herself, could live in a hostel; that she had enough education, didn't need more school; that she would be fine, didn't need anyone. She was very reluctant to have any help, saying that talking was a waste of time. When she stopped being defiant, angry, and self-sufficient, a very sad, fearful little girl could just be glimpsed. She was stuck either in denial, insisting she was fine, or in splitting those around into good—on her side—or bad—against her. If she had become more angry rather than argumentative and resentful, there was a danger she might have moved on to become aggressive and to damage people or property or begun to steal and lie.

The labels of "conduct disorder" or "oppositional defiant disorder" describe the behaviour but not the internal state. Underneath the behaviour, there is confusion, pain, and distress, with only immature ways of coping—splitting, denial, projection. But the mayhem the young person can cause can all too easily lead those around to confirm the young person's view of the world as hostile towards him/her.

Both parents were struggling to help their daughter and were united in their concern. Mother had a new partner who had tried to be a helpful parent, but the girl rejected him and was very rude. Mother and father both thought the move to live with father would help, but the girl remained difficult and out of control. Both parents were able to admit they had blamed each other and that their daughter had been offered privileges to be with them. The girl returned to live with her mother and new husband and visited father at weekends. Mother and father kept in close contact and were able to agree on what was acceptable in terms of pocket money, bed times, and school attendance. This was very difficult for these parents, but the risks to their daughter—who had been roaming the city late in the evening—helped them work together.

I hope this example shows the importance of trying to look beyond the behaviour and statements of the young person. What he/she might say or do, as in this case, can mask the underlying feelings; unless these are recognized, the parents' response may aggravate rather than help the situation. In more extreme cases the young person can be given a psychiatric label or an antisocial behaviour order (ASBO), but these do nothing for the actual emotional experience of the young person. If parents are unable to cope, help can be found at adolescent drop-in centres such as Open Door or the local Child and Adolescent Mental Health (CAMH) service via the GP.

It is more worrying when young people begin to show more fixed signs of such difficulties. They are too young for the label of a personality disorder—for example, Inadequate, Anti-Social, Schizoid, or Narcissistic personalities, which describe the presentation and the behaviour. Internally, however, each is a different means of coping with emotional pain and relationship difficulties, and changing this is a long, slow therapeutic process. Therapeutic work with young people is challenging and demanding, both for the professional and for the parents. The adults need to work together to trust that the other is doing the best they can and yet not become too involved. If the therapy starts as family sessions it may move on to family therapy, and this can be very helpful: matters that need to be shared can be talked over with the therapist as a neutral person, ensuring all the views and opinions are heard, that everyone has a chance to speak.

When the condition is severe, the therapeutic work is usually individual work with the young person and either some family meetings or separate meetings with the parents. The parents may have to make sure a reluctant young person attends, unless the young person decides he/she can attend alone. The content of the work needs to be given privacy, which can be hard for a parent who wants the young person to use the therapeutic time but then hears him/her declare it was a waste of time, or he/she didn't speak, or made some other denigrating comments. Mostly the therapeutic work proceeds in fits and starts, as painful issues, which are hidden, begin to emerge. At those times when the young person becomes angry or distressed, the parent may be left wondering whether therapy is helping. It is so important during these phases to encourage the young person both to continue and to have confidence in the outcome. Some parents need to talk over their concerns with a separate professional; during discussion about the young person, issues and conflicts from their own childhood may resurface. Parent work alongside the work with the young person can be extremely helpful, so that the parents have a place to work on their own emotional pain and then can have the emotional strength to parent the young person and support his/her treatment. Where this is not possible, the clinician seeing the young person may see parents at intervals.

Adolescence is also the time when differences that may have barely surfaced emerge. The gender difference is stark, but intellectual capacity is also more prominent.

A 12-year-old boy who had been cheerful and confident at his primary school after secondary transfer became increasingly withdrawn and low. He was aware he could not think as fast, learn as fast, or keep up with the other young people. His moderate learning difficulties were making him aware of his difference.

Young people who may have been diagnosed earlier on carry these differences into adolescence—for example, severe learning difficulties, autism, and physical illness such as diabetes, cystic fibrosis, hemiplegia, and epilepsy. Many then have to have help with anxiety or depression as they come to terms with their limitations and find ways to fulfil their potential. Much will depend on the quality of their relationships, currently and earlier. The body ego may have been accepted, but the young person is very vulnerable to the reactions of the family and of those around.

> A girl of 13 had, since birth, a paralysed leg and some limitation in the use of her arm. She became deeply depressed when her father suggested her leg be amputated and she be given a false limb. She felt she could be mobile with her crutches and was shocked that her father saw her as so disabled. She realized that her father felt guilty and perhaps ashamed and wanted to make it better with an artificial limb. She came to understand that he hoped for a magical transformation so that she would no longer be disabled. She herself had to face both his disappointment in her and her own denial of her limitations.

This rather dramatic situation highlights how it is sometimes more difficult for a parent to accept that a child has a disability than for the child him/herself. The daughter had had a traumatic birth with anoxia and was left with a hemiplegia. Father felt guilty and wanted to make it better or, rather, for it all to disappear and his daughter to be "normal". Parents may need help to accept their child's limitations, that they did not have a "perfect" child, when often the young person him/herself can say: "this is me, this is my body, this is who I am."

For other young people, previously unrecognized problems emerge with the demands of adolescence. Rheumatoid arthritis may start at this stage, or polycystic ovaries or other genital problems, rarely carcinoma of the testis—all problems such as these create fear and anxiety in the young person and anxiety and guilt in the parents.

Low mood

Young people can become anxious or depressed with low mood, a state of mind that may or may not have causes in the external world. The anxious young person may be anxious about everything (generalized anxiety), or there may be specific situations or events that provoke anxiety, leading to phobias or panic attacks. Anxiety can be a healthy normal response to a stressful situation, but when it is particularly disturbing to the individual and limits his/her life, then help is needed. Serious mental health concerns such as this, although more obvious and therefore more worrying, can respond to therapeutic help, but medication may sometimes be needed.

After transfer to secondary school, a rather obese girl of 11 years became anxious about swimming lessons and the teasing (or possible bullying) she experienced. This became overwhelming, and she refused to leave the house for fear of what would happen. She became tense, cried, and had tantrums if parents tried to force her. Then she developed panic attacks with sweating, tachycardia, trembling, dizziness, and fear of collapse. In her therapy she became aware of her anger and rage, her wish to attack and her fear of what others might do, and, beneath this, her distress and confusion about her identity and earlier life events that had been dismissed as insignificant. Slowly she became able to manage herself in her peer group, to think about her feelings and what she provoked in others. Her parents were not actively involved, except that father was able to talk about his problems at school and then to be more active in helping his daughter attend and manage. He took her swimming at the weekends, and she improved dramatically, becoming more confident.

Depressed young people can be very worrying—they can stop eating, have problems sleeping, and want to die or attempt suicide. But many of them mask their low mood by becoming angry, defiant, and difficult. Chronic low mood is not easy to relieve; acute depression is rather different: it is more overwhelming and frightening but does tend to recover spontaneously, even though there may be further episodes in the future. Some young people, without apparently being depressed, attempt to injure or kill themselves; they are worrying and more difficult to help, since they seem cut off from their feelings. Chronic depression involves low mood, feelings of hopelessness, fatigue, poor concentration, and low self-esteem. With therapy, they are slowly able to work through their vulnerability and despair and not retreat into a sense of giving up. Working with them therapeutically is a lengthy task; nothing is any good, nothing helps, and everyone easily becomes worn down. It is hard to engage and connect, as there is little trust and little belief that anything can change. Slowly reliability and consistency can build up some trust, and the young person shares some of his/her pain, confusion, and fear with the therapist and then, as progress takes place, begins to be able to talk to his/her parents or a close friend.

A young man of 14 living with his single mother was enraged with her and the lack of money, felt deeply hurt by his father's disappearance, was cut off and isolated at school, had no friends, and did not join in any activities. What slowly emerged was his sense that he was a useless, bad person who had caused father to leave and his longing to be valued and be valuable. It was very painful. After about a year of being seen once a week, he was doing well at school and had friends. His relationship with his mother was better, and he had accepted that perhaps in his twenties he could trace his father.

Major depression seems to be rather different: the young people have low mood, are angry and hopeless, but also have problems sleeping and eating. In therapy, they can often be silent or incoherent, and there is a terrible sense of an inner emptiness. They could easily cease to exist as they opt out of school and stay at home or in bed. There is a sense that the early relationships perhaps went wrong in some way and the young person has found it hard to move on and rebuild relationships using what the parents currently can provide. But many of these young people are very resilient, and, given time to struggle with these feelings, they can do it and allow themselves to grasp such relationships as are available now to rebuild their internal world. A small number of these seriously depressed young people go on to develop bipolar illness, with manic and depressive episodes. This usually emerges in older adolescents but can appear at this younger age. In these situations medication does seem appropriate alongside therapy. In a manic episode, the young person is excited and busy and tolerates frustration very badly. Their judgement goes, and they can embark on unrealistic activity and become intensely irritated when challenged; they talk and talk.

A young person of 14 started to wear flamboyant clothes and make-up, spending money he did not have. He was keen to change the world, and he joined various voluntary agencies, such as Greenpeace, but then fell out with them and started his own charity on the Internet. Reluctantly, he accepted therapy, and in this case he did slowly calm down. The limitations of his life—he had been adopted by elderly parents, and there was little chance of the media life he craved—was sad. Later, in a subsequent episode, he did need medication, and his parents helped him contact his local radio station and supported his efforts to become involved there.

As indicated earlier, when a young person has a serious mental health problem—in this case, bipolar or manic–depressive disorder—then a range of interventions is needed. This also can apply when the young person is clinically depressed but does not have the mood swings. Whether the young person needs medication, family therapy, or individual therapy or even a brief inpatient admission, the contributions of the parents and family are vital. Depression frequently runs in families, and so one or other parent may have some understanding of how the young person feels. But there is also, with this, a sense of guilt—"did I pass this on to my child?" Depression is multi-factorial: there are genetic factors, innate predispositions, but the emotional environment plays a large part, and then there are the individual circumstances and life events that impact on the young person and the family. Bullying at school is one such circumstance.

The role of the parents is complex, since they need to support the young person and keep him/her safe if he/she is taking risks or self-harming and must also manage their own possible guilt and depressive feelings. Parents may need help themselves to sort out what are their feelings, their own emotional issues, and what they are having to manage for the young person. The young person may be withdrawn and isolated or may talk for hours, often throughout the night. Parents need to be available and responsive, listening, or approaching and initiating interaction as appropriate, but above all they need to keep hopeful. The situation will improve, depressive episodes mostly decrease, and the situation improves. Then the parents need to encourage the young person to persevere with the therapy and, if advised, the medication. The depressive (or manic) episode passes but can recur or become chronic and low-grade. Therapeutic work offers the best chance of more long-term improvement. Often parents can be so relieved the depression has lifted that they want to "put it all behind them" and stop the painful therapeutic work. This would certainly be a regrettable development.

When parents themselves have been depressed or are depressed, it can be very helpful if they have therapeutic help in their own right, as a couple or individually. Young people when seen for review often comment that they are okay, adding "it is my parents who need the help now". Sometimes they are right.

Altered states of mind (psychosis)

Another mental health problem that can emerge in early adolescence is changing states of mind. This may be provoked by the use of substances or severe stress, but sometimes it is of unknown cause and may be linked to genetic factors.

A boy of 12 was convinced the water was being poisoned and refused to drink or have anything that tap water had touched. A girl of 13 felt that people were talking about her behind her back and that the people on the television were talking specifically to her. Both these young people responded to therapy: they were trying to make sense of their feelings and, as these were unbearable, evacuated their rage and vulnerability in their responses and attitudes to others. They were then left with the fear, as they felt that others were directing rage, poison, control back at them. It was not easy to manage their complex and overwhelming internal needs, fears, anxieties, and conflicts. Both these young people relied on their belief that they could be in control, could make sense of what they felt. This could be seen as omnipotence—"I can do it all, manage it all"—and this omnipotence has the capacity to help young people feel important even if under attack, so to give it up and be ordinary is hard.

Acute psychotic episodes or transient psychotic states need careful management, but the prognosis, the future outcome, is good. A young person experimenting with drugs, ecstasy, amphetamines, cocaine (crack), or the newer strong cannabis can become psychotic. The episode usually passes. The young person needs to be helped and may need medication, but more importantly he/she needs to learn to avoid substances that trigger psychotic episodes. Alcohol drunk to excess or when there is addiction can produce psychotic episodes, but the cause is clear and the need for moderation self-evident. This is quite rare in young people this age, as very few are addicted to alcohol. Of course, if illegal substances and alcohol are in frequent use in the home, then the young person may have easy access. To protect their young person, parents will then need to review how they are managing their own leisure activities.

Stress and trauma can produce psychotic-like states, similar to post-traumatic stress disorder, where there are flashbacks and the re-experiencing of phenomena; the young person relives the trauma and can appear to be almost psychotic. Stress and anxiety, if extreme, such as panic attacks or obsessive–compulsive states, can produce such fixed beliefs and such fear and terror that the young person has a virtual psychotic presentation. Parents are, of course, very worried and frightened by all these conditions and need help. They need to keep the young person safe and to obtain the therapeutic support and work they need alongside the interventions needed by the young person. Accessing help can be a worry in itself; the GP must be the first port of call, but there are also voluntary organizations such as YoungMinds, with a parent–help telephone service, NHS Direct, and Childline. Adolescent outreach services and early intervention in psychosis services are available in some areas. Parents need both to keep the young person safe and to persist in finding the help they need.

Where the psychotic episode is a precursor to schizophrenia, with problems with thinking and a reduction in movement (the young person may sit and stare into space), the situation is more serious. Medication in the form of the newer antipsychotics does seem to help, and as the young person stabilizes, psychotherapy helps him/her maximize what he/she can do. Many make considerable improvement, particularly if the home environment can be made less demanding emotionally and less conflictual. All these young people with serious mental health problems can benefit from regular and frequent therapy, both to stabilize their mental state and to help them find ways within their limitations of developing themselves and their lives. Parents also need advice and support.

A young person of 13 talked endlessly of the messages that came via the television telling her that she would be a big star and had a great figure and a great singing voice. She was isolated in school, the others labelling her as weird when seeing her talking to herself and smiling or laughing. She was of mixed heritage, and her black Jamaican father was a known schizophrenic. In therapy her fear of becoming like her father was palpable. She came across as deeply depressed, and then a switch would flick and she would be giggling, laughing, gyrating to a song she sang out loud or in her head. At times she could think and feel; at other times it was unbearable. She needed medication to help her bear the pain of her situation. It was recognized that she was really struggling, and her mother became actively involved in encouraging her school life and helping her with singing lessons. This young person did manage to become more realistic; she joined a local choir with her mother, and gradually the therapist slowly reduced her medication.

These examples show how complex the assessment of "psychosis" can be in young adolescents. True schizophrenic psychosis is rare at this age, and if this is the diagnosis then careful management with the use of medication and psychological therapy and family work can lead to improvement and a reasonable outcome. However, the diagnosis is painful and difficult for the young person and the family to accept, and it is also difficult for them to keep optimistic. The newer antipsychotics provide real advantages; they can greatly reduce the symptoms.

Other problems

Puberty is the time when eating disorders emerge, and they seem to be linked to the bodily changes taking place at that time. Many young people, mostly girls but some boys, find the body changes difficult, and many can become quite "well covered" or obese as the body changes. This is more likely with the excesses of modern diet.

Young people, individually or in a group, go on diets, and weight becomes a preoccupation. This may get somewhat out of control, and the young person becomes phobic about food, her periods can cease, and her body hair diminishes; for some, this can become overwhelming, and the loss of weight can be life-threatening. Many anorexics recover with age and maturity, but many need help; in therapy they struggle with issues of self-image, control, sexuality, and separation. Often they resist change, while apparently being compliant. They appear to work in the therapy and can appear to be trying to eat and behave differently, and yet in reality they hold fast to their view of themselves as too fat and find ways of disguising their refusal to eat by inducing vomiting or purging themselves. They appear to hear, comprehend, and agree with what is being explored, but nothing changes, or a little weight is gained, followed by panic and then weight loss. Seriously worrying anorexia probably needs inpatient help.

As mentioned earlier, in addition to anorexia nervosa, eating disorders include bulimia and food fads. Some young people are very picky about what they will eat, sometimes based on real concerns—"I am a vegetarian" or "I only eat fresh food". But others appear to live on sausages or bananas or lettuce and tomatoes and refuse anything else much. Food fads and anorexia are very difficult and frustrating for parents and cause tensions and scenes in the family. A family meal becomes a struggle as the young person picks at the food.

The person doing the cooking feels upset and hurt as he/she has probably tried hard to produce a pleasant, attractive, and nutritious meal. Both parents can become angry at the waste of good food, and siblings are unsure what to do and either refuse to eat also or rush through the meal to get away. Predictably, confrontations only lead to entrenched positions, and it may be more effective to resort to serving small portions. Certainly lots of encouragement can help.

With bulimia, the young person will eat and eat but then may be heard vomiting in the toilet. This, too, causes distress and anger in the parents. Of course, in all these cases the parents are really worried about the young person and afraid of what will happen next. If the situation does deteriorate, help is needed, starting with a careful assessment.

There are other conditions that may be recognized in the younger adolescent. Autism is nearly always diagnosed in childhood, but Asperger's may be recognized only in adolescence. Here there is impairment in social interaction, such as failure to make eye contact, a lack of empathy, poor peer relationships, and very poor emotional reciprocity, as well as restricted patterns of behaviour, such as routines or rituals and preoccupation with objects and activities. These young people may be distressed, or the concern may centre around them as they are totally immersed in Gameboys and other computer games.

Moody adolescents may, of course, also appear to be cut off and unaware, preoccupied with their own concerns, but this does not mean they have Asperger's syndrome. Normal adolescence includes periods of withdrawal and periods of extreme sociability. Concern needs to be raised in the minds of parents when a phase seems stuck and lasts for months and the parents realize that perhaps the young person has had difficult relationships and some worrying behaviours for some time.

At this age, the young person rarely seeks help for him/ herself; it is the families or schools that realize something is wrong. A group may help; individual therapy is not easy for the therapist or the young person and will probably need to last for years, Long-term help can enable the young person to maximize his/her potential and enable him/her to accept the limitations, Young people with Asperger's can slowly learn about emotions, feelings, and relationships, but it does seem learnt and comes across as laboured and artificial, rather than freeing up internal conflicted aspects of the self so that true feelings emerge; this only occurs in quite a limited way. It is slow, patient work. A group does more rapidly help the young people become aware of how they impact on others. They can learn strategies such as understanding the meaning of facial expressions.

In order to plan the most appropriate interventions for the young person, there needs first to be an assessment. Autism and Asperger's syndrome are now covered by the term Autistic Spectrum disorders, and there are a number of instruments/interviews that have been developed to help with the diagnosis. There are screening instruments and checklists usually completed by parents and then detailed interviews that are lengthy and deal with all aspects of the young person's life. This interview goes alongside observations of the young person him/herself, in the family and at school. The team of professionals who have assessed the young person discuss their findings, and a diagnosis is offered to the young person and family. Interventions are then planned together. (For further information, see Useful Publications.)

After two and a half years of intensive psychotherapy work, a young man of 14 said: "I know you are sad today" (true). "I can see it in your face and eyes but I don't feel it. You say and others say, 'I feel sad', or 'it feels as though you are sad'. I do not feel it. I do now recognize what I see in your face and eyes." It sounds as though he was denying his feelings, but there was a different quality: it was cut off, intellectual, a thing to be studied. There was no sense of the feeling being experienced.

Another common mental health problem of early adolescence is ADHD (Attention Deficit and Hyperactivity Disorder). The young person may need medication but also can improve with individual and family therapy. ADHD seems to be a combination of family environment, early disruption and trauma, and innate predisposition. These young people experience powerful feelings of rage and pain, which they are unable to process and manage. The feelings become overwhelming, and the young person feels out of control and frantically engages in activity to try to regain control. Their internal state is deeply confused and painful but the resort to action makes them hard to manage and work with in the usual therapeutic environment.

A boy of 10 rampaged in the consulting room: the curtains were pulled down, the wallpaper attacked, crayons went everywhere. The ball was used as a missile and then he left the room, running outside, kicking the ball, throwing it, and complaining. Back in the room everything was boring. For about a minute as he tried to write his name he focused and, as it went wrong, he looked despairing; then he was off again, climbing over the furniture and on the window sill. I was boring, persecuting, as I tried to set limits and was challenged as I tried to protect him, myself, and the room. It is not easy to persevere even when the child is likeable. The therapeutic work had to be moved from an ordinary consulting room to a therapy room with protected walls, window locks, and replaceable furniture. The play materials were limited to items that were less able to become missiles, and the work continued. The parents were helped to work together and to be clear about what was and what was not acceptable. They visited the school and the problems there were acknowledged, and a classroom assistant was assigned.

The therapeutic work progressed slowly as the anxiety and panic were explored. Medication was tried, but after three months with no change it was discontinued. The situation seemed to be improving, but transfer to the secondary school proved impossible, and at the age of 12 he transferred to a school with small classes where the young people did not move from classroom to classroom. He was able to recover and resume slow progress. The work with the parents proved crucial and continued throughout. When the boy was provided with individual help in the school, his outside therapy ceased.

For some young people with ADHD, medication can be very helpful, so it is worthwhile to have a trial period of it.

Less commonly, a young person may have obsessional compulsive disorder, which like ADHD, seems to be increasing— or to be increasingly diagnosed. The compulsions mean the young people can spend hours washing, tidying, sorting their clothes, putting their possessions straight, with numerous rituals that become ever more complex. Obsessive thoughts may go round and round in their mind, which they try to ignore, but they also become very fearful that if they cut across these thoughts or rituals something bad will happen.

A girl of 12 said, "I have to keep touching each rail on the fence and then wash my hands or something bad will happen to Mum. If I do it, that protects her." She knew this was irrational but was too afraid to stop. She feared that her mother might have another serious illness. In therapy, we explored the need for these rituals and why she needed to protect her mother. Her mother had had to go into hospital unexpectedly with abdominal pain, but this was dealt with smoothly. (A ruptured ovarian cyst caused the pain and an exploratory operation led to the removal of one ovary.) However, as the older child in the family, the patient blamed herself; she felt and expressed her fears that she and her younger brother were too much for mother, particularly when they argued or fought and mother shouted at them. During mother's hospitalization, she began the rituals of rail touching and the fear of germs and started frequent hand-washing. (They were encouraged to wash their hands before approaching mother in the hospital.)

These rituals had now gone on for about eighteen months, and she was felt by mother to be trying to control the family. Mother was understanding, but it became clear to her that they needed help when the girl had panic attacks if mother attempted to go out, having arranged a baby-sitter.

The girl was enraged that her mother had a new partner and a life of her own now; she needed mother to be home so she could feel safe. She only felt safe when mother, her younger brother, and herself were at home ,with the door bolted. When it was possible to think about her need to bolt the doors to keep her mother and brother inside, she began to understand her rage as a wish to keep the very close relationship she had with her mother and her pain that mother had a new partner. Slowly she had to face that she was still young, that she was not the protector: mother protected herself and the children. It was very painful to give up the sense she had of being powerful, but there was relief that she was not responsible. Slowly the rituals lessened; acceptance of the new partner was very difficult, but she did begin to make friends her own age and start to think of her own future.

Two conditions that may not appear immediately as mental health problems are enuresis (wetting in the day or at night) and encopresis (soiling with faeces). Most young people are clean and dry, but some have problems. They need to be checked for physical causes, but if no organic problems are found, it is very important to offer psychological assistance to the young person.

Soiling can be very embarrassing, and the young person is called names and becomes quite isolated. Wetting the bed at night can mean young people will not go on school journeys or sleep at friends' houses.

The young person and the family often have difficulty admitting there is a problem. Family sessions may lead to one of the parents admitting he/she had had a similar problem, and that parent may be able to help their young person. Often the family has problems sharing the bathroom, and this needs sorting out. Sometimes the young person finds it hard to express his/her feelings, whether it be anxiety or anger, and there seems to be a link with the loss of control. But many of these young people need individual work to help understand their feelings and the conflicts they experience and to help with reducing or, hopefully, resolving this distressing symptom.

Conclusions

Young people are on the threshold of independence and the need to move out of the family, make relationships, and manage their intense feelings of love, hate, sexual longing, loneliness, excitement, and joy. Many have anxious and difficult times, and some have particular problems. Where the difficulties are recognized and help is available, most can recover, and with support from their parents and perhaps an outside listening person—a family friend, a grandparent, aunt, or uncle, a school counsellor, or a telephone helpline—the developmental process can enable the young person to find some mental space and achieve a sense of well-being. The ones who struggle will need more intense and in-depth help.

It needs to be remembered that mental health problems such as those described in this chapter can occur more often if a young person has a serious, acute, or chronic physical illness or a disability. These young people may well need help from physicians and adolescent mental health teams, and the parents may need support and help to understand what the young person is experiencing and how they can assist him/her and also manage their own distress.

psychosocial issues

The impact of the environment on the young person is profound. Innate factors are clearly very important, particularly vulnerabilities that can emerge under certain conditions, but the dynamics in the family, the community, and the social setting, as well as his or her's current and past relationships, are all influential.

Relationships

The young person is a family member within a range of diverse family arrangements. Parents, step-parents, lone parent, siblings, step-siblings, half-siblings can be part of the family pattern, and how to find a place is not easy. Each young person has had earlier experiences, which are the bedrock; however, these attachments and internalized object relationships can be either supportive or undermining. Where a young person is anxious and enmeshed—that is, caught up with the parents so that he/she is emotionally preoccupied by whatever is the parents' view of the issue at that moment and does not have his/her own point of view—or is self-sufficient and avoidant of closeness, then he/she is likely to have difficulties at home and school. Parents need to find a way of dealing with the delicate balance between dependence and independence. The parents may well have conflicts with each other as they try to find the best approach. At times, they need to push the young person forward, encourage him/her to dare to take a risk; at other times, they need to hold the young person back to make sure he/she do not get out of his/her depth. And all the while they worry whether they are being over protective, and perhaps at times they will be. A parent may have mental health problems; there may be a depressed mother, or a father who drinks too much. The young person may withdraw, or he/she may take on the role of carer, helping the inadequate parent or replacing the dysfunctional parent in caring for siblings. The extended family may become actively involved, and the young person may either welcome this or feel surrounded by adults who make demands and set limits, but all the limits are different, resulting in confusion and conflict.

The young person's internal world is fluid and is in the process of renegotiating developmental stages and reworking unconscious conflicts. The internal objects and unconscious phantasies are very actively interacting, along with impinge-ments from the external world, so that explosions of rage and waves of distress are to be expected. Parents can usually manage to offer comfort during the distress, but they find the rage more difficult to manage. Family and friends, too, can more easily understand the distress and find the anger more difficult to understand. There are also surges of excitement at possibilities, with apprehension and longing around emerging sexual feelings and the delight at learning and intellectual creativity.

Bereavement

A death in the family can be a psychic shock: a grandparent may die, and the parent is plunged into grief, loss, and guilt. The young person may also be very sad, but it is more directly significant for the young person if a parent, sibling, or school friend dies. Mother may have breast cancer and die; father a heart attack; a sibling or school friend leukaemia. The internal world of the young person may feel fragmented, and he/she can become cut off and withdrawn or very depressed or appear to be indifferent. The process of mourning can be quite slow. If young people can talk to family members and friends over a year or so, they can slowly let the dead person die in their mind and retain memories of shared experiences. Then their energy and vitality can return, so that life can move forward. It is really important that the adults, despite their own distress, are able to listen to the young person. If a distressed, anxious parent tries to be helpful and tells the young people how they must be feeling and how they might manage it, then the young people may retreat further, since they can feel that the parent is in such a state of distress that he/she cannot afford to inquire how the young people feel. Young people report that they feel bothered because often they are more concerned about their parent or parents than they are about the dead person, and they feel bad that they are not so upset about the loss. It is often a while later that they themselves are upset about the loss.

A boy of 12 described how his mother died of cancer when he was 6 years old. The boy was tearful, depressed, and angry, getting into trouble at school because of his aggressive behaviour. He missed his mother every day and cried in bed most nights. He was stuck in a grief reaction and needed help. Initially, he had been very worried about his father and Grandma and did not miss his Mum: she had been ill in a chair for ages. But now he was very aware of the loss and longed for his Mum. He needed time to talk and to think about her with his father and on his own.

Divorce or parental separation

Many young people grow up in families where the parents have separated and perhaps have made new relationships, so the family is re-formed. Others have to live through the distress of parents deciding to separate, which is invariably a painful and difficult process for all involved. The adults are preoccupied, feeling full of rage and hate, hurt and rejected, and wanting to inflict revenge. Young people are only too aware of the demands on them; each parent wants loyalty and wants them to reject the other parent. There is probably a move of house and perhaps of school, leading to the loss of friends and neighbourhood, and perhaps also to a fall in the standard of living. Young people tend to react to parental separation by becoming contemptuous and dismissive, cutting off from the parent's distress. They spend more time out with friends and may give up on schoolwork and reasonable behaviour.

A girl of 14, who looked about 17, declared contemptuously that her parents were so busy trying to destroy each other that no one noticed or cared what she did. They had argued for years, and now they wanted to kill each other. Yes, she had stopped going to school and had tried stuff (cocaine), but, what the hell, she might as well have a good time—she could look after herself, she didn't need anyone, thank you.

Following the separation, and the divorce if parents were married, there is then the struggle over contact. The young person lives with one parent and may or may not want to see the other; the contact arrangements might also have been determined by a court. The loss of the regular involvement of the non-resident parent can be very painful, and visits are never the same. Parents may then find new partners, who may already have children, and there is another period of adjustment.

Parental separation or bereavement both result in the loss—by death or by geography—of a close intimate relationship.

The young person's world changes internally as well as externally. The relationship that was has to be mourned; emotional energy has to be used detaching from the internal object relationship in the internal world as well as the relationship in the external world. In the case of bereavement, the outcome needs to be a letting-go of the person and the internal object relationship and the retaining of memories. With parental separation, the person is still alive but the internal object relationships have to change for both parents, particularly the parent who has left.

Young people feel abandoned by deaths and rejected and betrayed by divorce; only gradually can they accept and to some extent understand. After parental separation, they need to establish a different relationship with the parent with whom they live and a very different relationship with the parent who has moved out. After this has happened, the resident parent may find that he/she has to manage the young person's anger and hostility, not only about the parental separation but also about the more routine frustrations and limitations of everyday life. The relationship with the non-resident parent may settle into a routine but may consist of more fun, with exciting and special times. Of course, if either parent begins another relationship and the young person has to get to know a new partner, then the relationships can shift again.

Where the parents are involved not only in fighting verbally but also in physical fights, then the consequences of this domestic violence are more serious for the young person. The fight may not have involved the young person, but witnessing the physical aggression might make him/her very fearful and watchful and have problems trusting anyone. Or the young person may him/herself become physically aggressive with siblings, friends, or the parents. Learning to manage anger and hate should begin in early childhood, but young adolescents need to relearn this. Their own violent feelings are very powerful, and violence enacted leaves them very vulnerable to repeating this. They may become victims if masochism prevails, or abusive or sadistic where there has been a lot of cruelty and their own aggressiveness has been able to grow unchecked. Just as the experience of a parent early on who can manage both his/her own feelings and help the child understand and manage his/her own feelings leads to the capacity to reflect, think, and have self-control, similarly young people take in from their parents an understanding of how pain and rage are managed in intense relationships.

Parents inevitably become angry with each other and at times become enraged. Hopefully, the parents can be angry but then calm down and discuss the problem and find a compromise way forward. Sometimes the rage becomes so fierce that there may be intense verbal abuse, even physical violence. In some families this can be quite frequent. Where the parents show little or no respect for each other in this way, the young person is exposed to the immediate distress and fear of their confrontation but can also learn that this way of expressing feelings is acceptable. Young people can then think that if they are feeling full of rage and hate, in the family or outside, it is alright to express this in a violent way, lashing out with words or physically. Some even enjoy the power that the physical or verbal strength gives them. Conversely, others see themselves as bad persons and accept being treated in this way. If they are verbally or physically attacked, it confirms their belief that they are useless, worthless. This is what can develop into a sadomasochistic cycle: a young person unable to manage his/her anger and hate becomes violent (sadistic); another young person feels guilty about feelings of anger and hate, seeing him/herself as bad or worthless, and becomes the victim (masochist); and together they have a relationship that is unhealthy for both of them.

Abuse and trauma

More obviously challenging and problematic than witnessing domestic violence is abuse of the young persons themselves. They may be subject to physical abuse—punching, beating, cigarette burns, knifing. Psychological and emotional abuse is when they are denigrated, undermined, criticized, and treated with relentless hostility; when their capacity to learn and think is mocked and sneered at, their self-esteem, self-worth, is demolished. Sexual abuse involves using the young person for the sexual gratification of the older person without regard to the appropriateness for the young person. This may involve penetrative sex, but it may also be touching inappropriately or more perverse acts involving urine and faeces.

Any of these abusive experiences (including the witnessing of domestic violence) lead to damage and distortion in the young person's internal world. The young people have had feelings aroused by what has happened, and these are difficult to manage. They all have overwhelming sensations of fear, anger, and excitement that they cannot process; some may be sexually excited. These feelings are not always converted into symbolic representations or words, and they can then only be registered as sensations. These sensations are stored in the deeper structures of the brain where the emotions are located. The result for the young person is that he/she may have a sense of something, an unpleasant or difficult feeling, but may not be able to name it or think about it. The experience can lead to a situation where there is a split between what is known and what is not known—that is, cannot be thought about. He or she is left in a state of confusion, unclear what or who is good or bad. If the abuser is a parent or other close supportive figure, then the discrepancy between the loved person and the damaging person can be difficult to manage.

The young person may be fearful and blame him/herself for events, for what he/she did or failed to do, which further lowers his/her self-respect. Young people may try to deny what happened, to believe that it didn't happen. Overwhelmed by the feelings and their attempts to manage them, they may project their feelings or sensations on to those around, who then become good or bad or who sense distressing material and in turn become confused. Young people find physical and sexual abuses very distressing as the body boundary is infringed and the abuser intrudes into their physical space. The body ego is very important in the sense of self of the young person. After such abuse, he/she may be left with post-traumatic stress disorder. The abusive experiences (physical, emotional, sexual) reappear as flashbacks or re-experienced phenomena, and the young person struggles to control these reappearances by avoidance, denial, or dissociation. He/she attempts to forget but frequently fails, and the experiences break through and surface.

Neglect—either physical or emotional—is also very damaging for young people. This is unlikely to start in early adolescence and so may have been present for some time. These young persons may well have failed to grow, have had frequent infections, and be functioning at a low level in school. Their overall development will be below their chronological age. Neglect is insidious; it can occur in the context of poverty and unemployment, but this need not be so. One child may be neglected in an otherwise well-functioning family.

A girl of 12 was pale and thin, with dark rings round her watchful eyes. Unlike her siblings, who looked healthy, she had mouth ulcers and herpes on her face; she was seen as slow at school and always tired. At home, she ate in the kitchen, washed and cleaned and looked after the family pets. She wet the bed and had to deal with her laundry and was kept near the downstairs toilet some nights. She asked to be taken into care: as the child of mother's earlier relationship the stepfather resented her presence, and she was treated as a servant.

If an adult or parent sees a young person who might be experiencing neglect, whether emotional or physical, it is not easy to find ways to help. In this case, the mother asked for help partly because the school had expressed concern. If the adult is a family friend or relative, then often spending time with the young person, taking an interest, and allowing him/her to talk can be helpful. For a non-resident parent, it is extremely difficult because criticism is easily perceived, even where none was intended. But often it is possible to explore whether anything can be done to help, such as offering respite so that the young person has weekends away, or perhaps holidays and half-terms.

This particular girl went to a boarding school funded by the local authority and made good progress. Last seen she was more robust physically, was learning in school, was more confident, and had made friends. The plan was that she would return to live at home full-time after GCSEs.

Substance abuse

Where the situation at home is difficult or where they are very restricted, young people can be attracted by the alcohol and illegal drug scene out in the community. This seems to provide excitement, a group of friends, and an anaesthetic for the pain and futility of existence. The existential questions of "who am I?" and "why am I here?" can be avoided. The conflicts, distress, and pain of the internal and external worlds are eliminated, for a while. Once addicted, then obtaining more stimulants becomes the dominant goal. Attempts to engage these young people in helping schemes are frustrating. Consumption is denied or reduced in quantity, and underlying issues are dismissed. Lying and stealing have no meaning and are undertaken without compunction. Money is needed for the required alcohol and/or drugs.

Once parents realize that their young person is using substances or alcohol, generally they become very concerned. Of course, if there are substances or alcohol in the home, these need to be removed or kept secure. It is important to take time and explore with the young person what he/she has been taking, where, and with whom. Many young people experiment with substances because of both curiosity and peer-group availability. If the peer group regularly uses substances or alcohol, then parents need to think how to limit their use and frequency but may have to accept some involvement.

The situation becomes worrying if the young person is actively seeking out alcohol or substances and is, in effect, self-medicating to deal with distress and emotional conflicts that he/she cannot manage. If the use of alcohol or substances is having negative consequences such as lying, stealing, falling behind at school, or non-attendance, then serious measures must be taken. If he/she has lost control and is psychologically or physically dependent on the substance or alcohol, then clearly the situation is very serious and parents will need to seek help. There are limited services—some outpatient, some day-patient—in the state sector; most of the inpatient services are in the independent private sector. Alongside managed withdrawal or reduction of substance use there needs to be the offer of counselling or therapy, and the parents themselves need support and advice; both are often available in the voluntary sector. Publications for drug-related early-intervention services for young people and families, as well as other publications, can be found in the Useful Publications section.

Refugees and asylum seekers

There are now many young people in Britain who have lived through natural disasters, wars, and persecution in their country of origin. They are often alone or are with a distant family member only. They may have post-traumatic stress disorder, be depressed and confused, and be very behind with their education. Language is likely to present difficulties, and there may not be the opportunity to pursue their original religious beliefs. They need help with interpreters and cultural advisors, as well as for their mental health issues. If they have witnessed family members dying, killed, or tortured and slaughtered, they may be in shock, unable to think or feel.

A 13-year-old girl from Zaire described through her interpreter seeing her parents decapitated with machetes and her grandmother raped and killed; she also had no idea where her sister was now. This young girl was in a foster home and attended a school where many other refugees were placed. She attended a group in the school and was seen with her foster-family to think about her panic attacks and nightmares. When she had settled and learnt some English, she had individual sessions to help with the emotional distress. Lawyers and social workers tried to clarify her position and the future.

Interventions

All these young people who have been abused or traumatized need help. Often this will need to be over a prolonged period, although talking things over initially can be helpful if the memories are very vivid in their minds. Often they are very afraid they are going mad. As the emotional impact emerges after the shock, then individual or group therapy is needed;

additionally, work with whoever is providing care may be important. A traumatized young person can be difficult to live with, rude and angry, or silent and withdrawn; he/she may go out, wanting to avoid thinking, and resorting to sexual relationships and substances such as alcohol. The parents and carers need support and help alongside the help for the young person. It is very important that the parents or carers do not give up on him/her but remain hopeful and persist. Were they to give up, then the young person would be left feeling angry and helpless.

Conclusion

Sadly, psychological problems are increasingly common. Growing up is always stressful, but when the adults around—either in the family, or the local community, or the wider community—are in a state of turmoil, then natural disasters have to be accepted; however, man's inhumanity to man leaves young people struggling. When the adults have not learnt to manage their own rage, hatred, fear, and sexuality, then the young people are both victims and also lack internal and external models—objects—to help them manage their own intense feelings.

6

parents

Given that adolescent turmoil is normal in young people aged 10 to 14 years, then it also has to be a given that parenting these young people is stressful and challenging. The young person may be your own child or perhaps an adopted child, a step-child, or a foster-child, and some young people are in residential care such as boarding schools or children's homes, but they can all be demanding and difficult as well as a delight.

As the child moves into puberty and becomes adolescent, the "parent" has to face and deal with a number of issues. The young person's intellectual development means he/she argues about and discusses everything. Young people may become involved in issues such as global warming, globalization, or animal rights and be intensely and passionately convinced that they are right. Others become vegetarian and cause difficulties in household management as well as with their ideas. Yet others become immersed in computer games or the Internet. All of these interests create a person who is hard for adults to embrace fully, even when the causes are those that the whole family accepts.

Alongside these passions, there are increasing pressures from school and the examination system. Some young people flourish in this environment; others flounder and need encouragement and support. Now is the time when young people have to confront their strengths and weaknesses; their failures can be painful for the parents, as parental dreams are also fragmenting.

Young people are also dealing with their blossoming sexuality and having early intense same-sex and/or opposite-sex relationships. The peer group's views and attitudes may cut across those of the family, which can be conflictual. Some other young people avoid relationships and retreat from friendship, and this can cause great concern to parents.

Parents know they need to be supportive and encouraging while retaining responsibility and setting appropriate limits. This is difficult, as any confrontation can be intense and the hatred hard to bear. As the young person matures, he/she has to gradually have more scope, take more risks, and learn from his/her own mistakes. But when a young person is at times an apparently competent 18-year-old but at others apparently 3 years old, the judgement is stressful. A parent can never get it right—just sometimes it is good enough. Where there are two parents or parental figures, it is very helpful if they as adults can have clear and shared views. They will need to discuss afresh their principles, self-control, and morality, for example. This is most important so that they can deal with situations such as when there are fights or bullying at school and they need to help their young person protect him/herself and manage the situation; sexual exploration with his/her peer group, which may be same-sex or opposite-sex; and leisure-time activities, which may include parties where there is experimentation with intoxicating substances.

The young person may also raise broader issues that the parents have cause to be concerned about, such as the building of new roads, or cutting down trees to make space for houses to be built, or religious belief and becoming an active member of a faith community. Parents can never be fully prepared, but it is important to be consistent and to agree together the approach to take if this is possible. If parents do each have different views, these need to be acknowledged and the differences discussed; the young person must be encouraged to develop his/her own ideas and not feel pulled into an alliance with one parent against the other.

Above all, parents of young adolescents need endless patience and time. At 11.00 pm when the parent is exhausted and ready for bed, the young person will want to talk—about relationships with friends at school that have gone wrong, despair about the future, anxiety about homework, longings for a new electronic piece of equipment or to be in the school team or for a particular boy and girl to be their friend.

It can be very difficult. A parent could all too easily say, "I have been here all evening or all weekend, and now I am too tired—can we talk tomorrow?" But tomorrow the young person will probably be withdrawn and cut off again. It does seem important if possible to find the energy at the time to listen to the young person and to try to help. This means being empathic, understanding the young person's distress, but also helping him/her regain a sense of perspective. Hopefully, the young person then feels understood and can also recognize that, although it may be painful, the current dilemma is not the end of the world.

Not your own child

There are many children who, for a number of reasons, are no longer living with their birth parents. As the young person grows physically and develops emotionally he/she will experiment, and when he/she starts behaving in a way that is reminiscent of a birth parent who may be feared or hated by the carer with whom the young person is now living, then this psychological parent can become shocked and horrified. Adoptive parents or step-parents are always anxious that the young person is going to "revert to type", and this can create more complex conflicts. The young person may be identifying with the absent parent and may fear adulthood, may fear, for example, that she too may become mentally ill like her birth mother. Where the birth parent was promiscuous or was criminal, this too can be anticipated and feared by the psychological parent.

It is never easy deciding when to share with a young person information about his/her birth parent. In times of despair or conflict, all too easily the young person or the new parents think that the same path is inevitable. If it is discussed, then many fear that it will direct the future and is almost bound to happen. If it is not discussed, the young person senses the uncertainty and reacts to this. Sadly this can also lead to him/her enacting what was feared. Attempts to protect the young person and steer him/her in a particular direction may, in fact, result in the opposite response. If the family can talk about what is known about the birth parent and an understanding of how this happened, then the young person can, hopefully, continue the conversation when situations trouble or perplex him/her. The essential thing is not to throw at the young person what is known about the birth parent as a form of attack or criticism. To be told "you are just like your father/mother" can only drive the young person further away.

Single parents

Bringing up an adolescent alone is very hard work. Inevitably in a family, there will be fights and confrontations, and two parents can share the barrage. If the single parent has to cope with the rage and fury and then take the supportive caring role, the demands on his/her emotional resources will be very great. Recharging the single parent's own emotional reservoirs is very important. His/her own support systems, parents, extended family, and friends are essential, and if he/she is working and running the home, physical energy can be fully stretched in addition to the emotional depletion. Choosing which issues to turn into a battleground and which to let go needs careful consideration, and consistency helps the young person to accept and internalize the limitations.

Single parents draw on their own childhood experiences and the loving and supportive relationships they have had to ensure they retain their sense of themselves as a worthwhile valuable person—as the young person in a rage screams "you are rubbish, useless, cruel and a complete failure!" Many single parents are able to take on the bringing up of their children with energy, enthusiasm, and enormous commitment. With a network of family and friends the young people should flourish, but it is tough at times and the parents' own supportive relationships are therefore important.

Some single parents become very devoted to their children, so that the children become their *raison d'être*. This can feel good for both, but it is important for the parent to have an outside life—not just work, but also a social life and important relationships. This is not easy, but the children, who will have their own friends and a life outside the home, need to feel that one day they can leave and the parent will be all right. The parent therefore needs to have the benefit of outside support and stimulation for his/her role as a parent but also needs to have a life of his/her own that will continue when the children leave home.

The corporate parent

Young people in care, whether in a foster family or a residential unit, usually have a history of abuse or trauma. During adolescence the effects of this come to the surface, and carers can consciously or unconsciously fear/expect the young person to become abusive or a victim again.

The young people can be very determined to be independent, wanting to make decisions for themselves about where they live and where they can go. Social workers and foster parents who share the care of a particular young person struggle to be supportive but also to set appropriate limits, and conflicts frequently occur. These conflicts can often mirror the original traumatic situation and need careful reflection before action.

For example, a foster carer may see a young person as defiant and impossible and want him/her to be removed and placed elsewhere. The social worker may see the young person as vulnerable and misunderstood. Both of these aspects are true and reflect the young person's relationships with a father who abused and a mother who attempted to protect. Moving the young person without an attempt to work on these responses does not help. The young person who is being defiant is unconsciously being provocative with the foster parents to see if they will react in the same way as the abusive father did. So if these issues can be discussed and the foster parents understand what is happening, then the need to move the young person can diminish.

Parents' own issues

A young person's adolescence frequently coincides with developmental steps for parents.

Father may begin to realize he has reached as far as he can professionally, and this may be disappointing or humiliating. In order to compensate he may seek to boost his self-esteem and to find excitement in a challenging hobby such as mountaineering or motorbikes, or he may retreat to the pub; an affair, with the accompanying sexual excitement, can be very attractive. All these activities can be seen as attempts to cope with internal distress. Mild to moderate depression is common, and men who have had little time for feelings and emotions may have problems now when action is not always the solution. The sexual relationship with the mother may be in a difficult phase or have become routine and boring, and this may also contribute to internal doubts and anxieties about ageing. Other fathers may, however, have finally overcome their anxieties and uncertainties and may become more lively, more involved, and more available emotionally, which can be a joy and delight to the family.

Mother very often begins to move into the menopause during her children's adolescence. Hot flushes, poor sleeping, and mood swings can be difficult when a young person is very demanding. Mother has to face her own ageing and decline, and the young person is blossoming into an attractive, beautiful young thing. Sexual tension can be very evident, and mother may be well aware that her sexual needs are changing and erratic. If the mother becomes depressed she can withdraw even more from her partner, and this creates further conflict.

A mother who has been working may find that as the children become more independent, she can become more involved at work, which increases her confidence and self-worth. If she moves up the career ladder and becomes better paid and more able to make decisions and carry responsibility, then this has an impact on the family and mother's relationships as she becomes more assertive and independent.

Adult relationships during these transitions are very stressed. Both parents may have views on how to respond to the young person's needs and demands, but the parents' views may be very different from each other's, drawing from their own childhood experiences. It may be that at such times the parents need to step back and that successful parenting means less involvement with the young person, but still being available for him/her.

The importance
of a parent's own childhood

As indicated throughout, the parenting that the parents, adoptive parent, or foster carer bring to their role of parent depends in large part on their own early experiences with their parents. Their earlier feelings, conflicts, and experiences and how they react to these are therefore crucial in the here-and-now, dealing with current concerns. The adults themselves will be aware of the current issues—social, financial, and political—that the family unit is facing but may be less aware of their own internal issues. Their early experiences with their own parents and circle of family and friends will have provided pleasure, joy, and hope but may also have aroused rivalry, jealousy, and destructiveness. These negative feelings may have been accompanied by despair and hopelessness.

Young people who are in the grip of their intense feelings tend to want to be rid of them and behave in such a way as to leave the adults around feeling hopeless and helpless. If the hurt or rage or despair connects with the adults' own internal feelings, then the adults may find they have feelings that overwhelm them. In such circumstances, the vulnerable parent needs a partner—or close friend, if a single parent—for support, so that he/she can regain his/her perspective on what is to do with the young person and what is his/her own internal issue.

A slim, attractive 13-year-old girl attacked her mother for her dress sense and for her figure, her large hips. The mother, aware of a beautiful sibling of her own as a child that she could never match, ended up in tears when her partner confirmed that she was badly dressed and unattractive. In such circumstances, the young girl was left triumphant but also anxious and worried about her own future development as an adult woman. The partner needed to think about his own ageing and rivalry with his younger, more sporty and academic brother. The family needed joint sessional work, but the parent couple also needed space to share their childhood pain again now they were in "middle age". Only then could the young girl be free to do the developmental work she needed.

Young people need a parental couple that can stand pretty solidly for them to kick against. Parents may disagree but need to be able to discuss their differences and reach a compromise. When this does not happen, the young person can drive a wedge between them. He/she may appear to want this as he/she develops a close relationship with mother or father, but in fact this is unhelpful for the young person, who needs to learn about negotiation and compromise and what the limits and standards should be. If the parental relationship breaks down, the young person can become trapped in the relationship with one parent, and then separation is not easy.

In a chapter in *Partners Becoming Parents* (Clulow, 1996), Phillip and Carolyn Cowan describe how they work with parents to help them through this process and look at the impact on children and young people of these transitions in relationships. Another chapter, thinking about step-parents, by Margaret Robinson, describes her understanding of the challenges new partnerships face. What emerges is the demands and difficulties of parenting and of sustaining an adult intimate relationship. Couples need to work over a lengthy period to be able to understand what each brought to the situation and how they might need to develop both their understanding and their strategies to cope together with the young person. The conscious and unconscious issues in a couple need to be brought to the surface and discussed in detail. The young person can disrupt the communication systems on a conscious level and also affect the unconscious projections that sustain the parental relationship. The exhaustion produced by a young person who needs to talk or argue at midnight can also make adult relationships very fragile.

It is worth considering whether at times the young people are being used by the parents in their own conflicts. The young person may be a victim used by one parent to hit out at the other—"she is just like you, selfish." Some young people who become very argumentative at midnight have been used as a parental confidant and ally. They may also sense the parental conflict and, by behaving outrageously, try to keep the parents together, united against their "impossible adolescent"!

Finding a way

Parents often need to spend more time together, rather than less, when they are parenting adolescents. The young people are more able to manage, and parents can rediscover their social life, although finding an adult to be responsible for the young person is still required. Shared interests have to be rediscovered or new interests developed. But the most important use of time is to spend time talking over conflicts and the young person's demands, alongside finding time to sustain and enjoy an intimate marital relationship.

If all is fundamentally well between the adults, the young people sense this and, despite their rage, know there is a secure base. If the relationship is disintegrating or breaking down, the young person knows or senses this, and his/her sense of a secure base gives way to anxiety and probable further challenging behaviour: clearly, these are issues that need to be discussed. Many parental couples need help, from a mediator, counsellor, or therapist (Tsiantis, 2000); most use family or friends, while a few, sadly, give up and seek consolation elsewhere. But the break up of the relationship should not be the end—joint parenting should continue even if the partnership breaks. Talking and discussing parenting issues will need to continue.

Conclusion

Parenting adolescents is very demanding, and many parents need support and help. Small children are demanding physically, but adolescents challenge every aspect: physical, emotional, and intellectual. But they are also great fun as they are interested in everything and are curious and able to be creative. A sense of humour is essential for parents.

interventions

Young adolescents are often reluctant to seek help; when they do, they may only be willing to be involved briefly. Unlike older adolescents , only a very small proportion of young adolescents needs medication or intensive treatment as inpatients. What many of them benefit from, if they can allow themselves to accept it, is some form of psychotherapy or talking treatment.

Talking things over

Many young adolescents are able to talk about problems to their parents, to a member of the extended family, or to a family friend. Others talk to a teacher or a teaching assistant or the parents of a school friend. If these adults have some understanding of mental health and psychological well-being, they can allow the young person to talk and work out his/her own way forward. Sometimes he/she needs advice, and the adult can outline options so that the young person has a wider view of the possibilities. Just occasionally, the adult may need to actively intervene if the young person is at risk, such as from a serious eating disorder, abuse, serious drug use, self-harm, or other ways in which his/her mental state is threatened.

Situations such as these cause great concern to parents, the extended family, and friends, and all of them also worry that they are interfering, being over-anxious. Hopefully, the parents will be able to talk their concerns over with each other and with their network to clarify whether the worrying behaviour is something more than normal adolescent turmoil. If, for example, the young person is losing weight even if he/she appears to be eating adequately though on a diet, or if a usually lively and argumentative young person starts to withdraw, then patience is needed to encourage him/her to talk over what he/she is feeling. It is also important for adults to take seriously what is being said. Young people who have been abused, or bullied, frequently report in therapy that they tried to tell a grown up that things were wrong, but they did not find the grown up very receptive to their approaches.

If a young person, contrary to his/her usual behaviour, becomes easily angry and flares up at home or at school, getting into trouble, it is worth considering whether the cause might be depression. Depressed young persons, when they are being irritable and touchy, will confirm feeling low and sad. However, anorexic, bulimic, or substance-abusing young persons will hide what is happening and can be very wary and rejecting of offers of help, and in these cases parents need to be very vigilant. There are telephone helplines where parents can seek advice; there are also self-help groups that provide information and support.

Consent and confidentiality

If these services do not prove sufficiently able to help the parents, they may need to seek professional help, perhaps first talking to the school and then visiting their GP. If it is felt appropriate, the young person and the family will be referred to the local CAMH service. Many young people refuse help or advice initially but later, as things are explained and they calm down, will agree if the parents and general practitioner are suggesting a course of action such as a joint meeting or a referral.

There are very considerable issues around consent and confidentiality for these young people, and the whole area needs to be handled sensitively. Parents remain legally responsible for their child until he/she is 16 years old. (If the young person has been in care at any time or has a disability, parents are also deemed responsible until age 18 or 19 years.) This responsibility also applies to step-parents, adoptive parents, foster parents, and the corporate parent (the local authority).

However, below age 16 years, and under certain circumstances, a young person may legally seek medical help and accept an intervention without parental consent. This was established following a legal challenge as to whether a doctor could prescribe contraception to a girl under the age of 16 years without the consent of her parents (*Gillick v West Norfolk & Wisbeck Area Health Authority*). After appeal, the final ruling was that young people of sound mind who have a full understanding can consent to their treatment—be it contraception, medication, or a talking treatment—without their parents' knowledge or in spite of parental objections. This ruling is known as Gillick Competence.

All this will need to be explained and understood by the young person, as well as by the parents. So there is a distinction between consent and refusal in the law covering young people. Young people of sound mind and understanding can consent to their own treatment; but if parents and the practitioner decide an intervention is essential, the young person cannot refuse. Of course, it is sensible to encourage young people to inform their parents if they are having any treatment. However, if a young person is thought to need help—perhaps to be fed if anorexic or given antidepressants and psychological therapy and kept safe if seriously depressed and suicidal—then even if the young person refuses, the parents can consent and the help is given. In an emergency, such as diabetic pre-coma or after an overdose of tablets, the doctor can act even if the young person refuses and no parent is found in sufficient time. In summary, young people under 16, if considered to be aware and to understand the situation, can consent to treatment, without the consent of their parents. But young people cannot refuse treatment; parents or medical staff can overrule their wishes. It needs to be remembered that if parents are divorced and the non-resident parent has shared "parental responsibility", then both need to give consent, not just the parent with whom the young person lives.

(Between 16 years and 18 years, the situation is more complex; agreement of the young person—and preferably the parents—is needed if help is offered. The young person can refuse and cannot be overruled; however, medical staff are advised to take legal advice if they and the parents consider an intervention is vital, and it will then be as the court decides.)

Involving social services

If the situation deteriorates too seriously between the young person and the parents—perhaps the young person is alleging abuse, or the situation at home is very difficult because of domestic violence or alcohol problems, or there is a serious breakdown in communication—it may be that social services need to become involved. This situation may become apparent when for some reason he/she goes into hospital or if he/she refuses to go home after school, for example. The parents themselves may feel that the young person is out of control, prone to violent angry outbursts, or perhaps is using alcohol or other substances and does not respond to the parents' attempts to help. Social services can provide support and short-term respite or longer term placements, as an emergency or on an Interim Care Order under the Children Act. If the young person has become disturbed, perhaps after using illegal drugs, or is seriously depressed, then help under the Mental Health Act can be accessed. The GP is important if this is a possibility, to advise and initiate the process.

In most cases, however, the law does not need to be involved. Outreach teams from health and social services can provide treatment and support in the home; then, when the situation settles, the outpatient services can be put in place.

All of this is very difficult for parents, and they may need to ask for professional help themselves or be supported by family and friends. At some point, family work is often part of the intervention; this can be painful but is usually very helpful. The young person may well need longer term individual help after the crisis is over.

Community resources

Other young adolescents may need community resources if their immediate home and school environment does not contain anyone they feel comfortable to have as a confidant. Youth clubs and faith centres often have access to counsellors, and GPs also often have counsellors. Young people are very reluctant to visit their doctor, but some practice nurses have links with schools and local facilities for young people. There are a number of organizations in the voluntary sector that have centres for young people. These may be based around an activity such as chess or a range of sports—football, rugby, swimming—and these groups can provide other young people and adults to talk over issues.

More specific drop-in centres for young people are available in some places, often in the voluntary sector. Young people need parental consent if they are to be seen regularly but can be seen for consultations in their own right. There are a number of psychotherapies, and young people often have an idea themselves what will be useful for them. If they have a specific problem, they can be clear they want help with that, and a brief cognitive behavioural intervention can be appropriate. Then the young person moves on, knowing he/she can come back. Problems that can be helped in this way could include fear of travelling, some panic attacks, and some problems in school, such as bullying. Many young people are reluctant to be seen alone—a one-to-one with an adult is unbearable for them—but if there is a group available, they may find this more acceptable. Young people may be seen in general groups, where the participants may have a range of problems; others may be in specific groups, where all the participants have similar problems, such as all with diabetes, all with cystic fibrosis, or all with divorcing parents. The relationships between the young people and between them and the group leaders provide an excellent way to bring about change in the young persons' understanding of themselves and their impact on others. The leaders need to be experienced in managing the intense feelings generated and using them to promote the emotional health of the young people.

Family work

If the young person is experiencing particular problems in the family, then family work or family therapy can be helpful. This may be in a community centre or a specialist setting. At all times, the involvement and support of the parents is essential.

The family work may have a particular focus—for instance, fostered and adopted children have issues, as do their parents, and working on attachment issues can be helpful. The children and parents in these situations find adolescence very stressful as they try to understand the past and not be unrealistic about their expectations of each other.

Formal family therapy can enable difficult areas to be faced and worked on. As the issues are often very painful, this does need well-trained, well-supervised therapists to facilitate, contain, and manage the process.

If parents become concerned and feel their communication with the young person and perhaps their discussions about the young person are becoming too tense and strained to manage, it does help to seek outside involvement. There are voluntary organizations such as Open Door in North West London or the Kensington Consultation Centre in South West London. The Citizens Advice Bureau (www.citizensadvice.org.uk/index/getadvice.htm) or the local general practice will have a list of such organizations. YoungMinds can also help to suggest what might be available in any area.

Therapy

In the case of a young person who has serious difficulties that are distorting his/her development either emotionally or psychologically, then individual psychodynamic psychotherapy can be very helpful. For most young people, this will be once weekly; just occasionally it needs to be more often. This therapy does not address specific problems directly; rather, young people are allowed to tell their therapist what is bothering them and gradually to build up a relationship that can then be used to show them how, within the consulting room, they often repeat situations from the past or in their current life. Gradually they feel understood and also develop an understanding of how they function and how this leads to their difficulties. They are then able to recognize that they do have choices and some responsibility, therefore, for what happens.

Psychodynamic, psychoanalytic psychotherapy is not a quick fix and can often need several years. But there are therapeutic interventions that can be much shorter. Some services offer a brief consultation service, of up to five sessions. This does need well-trained, experienced, well-supervised therapists; often young people at the point of a crisis can use these sessions to reflect and consider the way forward. They are in a psychically fluid state, and the opportunity to talk things through can give a deep understanding that is surprising. Many can then move forward by themselves.

Another, longer form of brief therapy is one that has been used for specific problems. Such help may be available from CAMH service clinics, or specialized projects run by voluntary agencies, such as NCH or NSPCC. The following study illustrates this form of therapy:

Girls who had been sexually abused, many of whom were young adolescents, were offered up to thirty sessions of individual psychodynamic psychotherapy or up to eighteen sessions of group therapy. The parents or substitute parents were offered sessions in parallel with the work with the girls. Many of these girls were deeply troubled; they had suffered contact—mainly penetrative sexual abuse—and many were still suffering from post-traumatic stress disorder. About half were clinically depressed and anxious.

Where the girls were offered individual psychodynamic psychotherapy, the parents or foster parents were seen alongside the work with the young person. Many of them valued the opportunity to talk about their problems in looking after the girl and keeping her safe. Many acknowledged they had been in difficult relationships and regretted letting the situation continue. Others were able to talk about their own difficult childhoods and how their own depression and preoccupation had prevented them from paying more attention to their daughter. In the same way, the girls in the individual psychodynamic therapy were preoccupied not by the abuse they had experienced, but by issues in their families. Loss, disruption, and change were the issues for them: the mothers of some had died of breast cancer; other girls had moved house and school or gone into foster care. The pain and distress of these events was overwhelming but could be thought about and shared. The abusive experiences needed to be acknowledged but were mainly not the most significant issue. In this individual work each child could raise and explore what the issues were for her, and most of them improved. (For a full description of this study, see Long & Trowell, 2001.)

This study is included here to illustrate how important it is to talk about painful and distressing events when they happen. And how important it is for parents to try to find ways of managing their own past pain and distress so they can be available emotionally for their children and young people.

There are always going to be very painful events, deaths, serious illnesses, and upheavals, which badly damage relationships between people and leave distress behind. But what is important is to know that they can be worked on so the pain can lessen—switching off does not work long-term, and sinking into despair is also destructive.

Young people need parents who are alert, in touch with their feelings, and available emotionally who can talk and think about painful situations and manage the anger that may also be provoked. Perhaps parents need to think about whether they themselves need support, counselling, or therapy to help them parent well. This is particularly important if they had distressing childhood experiences or their relationship with their partner is problematic.

In the group therapy offered to abused young people, described above, there had to be an agreed topic for each session, alongside work in the relationships in the room. The young people were able to share their experiences and improve their capacity to interact with others. They no longer felt isolated in their experience and "secret", but their specific issues from their own situation were less easily addressed. Most of these young people also improved. Alongside these groups, the parents and foster parents also had support and help, and similar issues emerged. These parents, too, recognized they needed help long before the abuse became the concern.

Some of the young people who attended either type of therapy did subsequently need more long-term individual help. What they had been offered provided immediate relief, but to build up enough trust and have sufficient understanding of themselves and others, they did need more long-term therapy. The parents welcomed this, as they recognized that the young people had progressed but needed more therapeutic input.

In another multinational project (Trowell et al., 2007), depressed young people—boys and girls of 10 to 14 years of age—were offered up to thirty sessions of individual therapy or up to fifteen sessions of family therapy. Where the young people were seen individually, the parents were offered work in parallel. These young people were depressed for a range of reasons. Some came from families where there was a long history of depression, in parents, grandparents, and extended family. Many were currently living in single-parent families or in families where the parents were at war or were divorcing. All the young people in the London part of the project had major problems in school and were not learning; most were not attending school. The young people seen individually were deeply troubled but most were surprisingly well able to use the sessions and to get back into school, learn and move on in their lives. Similarly in family therapy, the young people improved, although they could have benefited from a longer intervention or a top-up session. A few families could not cope with family therapy and dropped out of the intervention. It is not known what happened to these families as, sadly, they refused subsequent offers of help from the local services.

> What emerged strongly from this project was that these children were living in families with seriously depressed and troubled parents. These adults needed help. The young people could use the help offered and get on, leaving their troubled parents in the hands of the professionals. Again the parents were able to acknowledge that they had not been able to manage well. Some had current marital conflicts, others had troubled and distressing early experiences themselves. They wanted help now but expressed some regret at not seeking help sooner themselves.

Young people have a range of interventions available. It is important to recognize that young people dip in and out and that what they need at one point may be different from what they need later. They need a range of duration as well as of intervention type. Some respond to a one-off consultation, some to five sessions, some to a nine-month treatment plan, whereas others need long-term open-ended therapy. They are mainly well able to use what is available—they have the developmental process on their side.

Other interventions

Parents have a real dilemma when their young person needs help. It is a matter of trying to find out what is available in their area. CAMH services accessed via the GP may be the right service. But there are counselling services and drop-in services that young people may find more acceptable—for example, Open Door, or the Brandon Centre (in Kentish Town: www. brandon-centre.org.uk). The GP should know what is available locally. Independent psychology services are available, as well as those attached to organizations such as Barnardo's or NCH (Action for Children); YoungMinds has a directory that may be helpful, as well as a Parents Information Service phone line.

Parents who recognize they need help can approach Relate or the Tavistock Marital Studies Institute. There are also independent services available, and again the GP may be able to help.

There is, of course, a range of other interventions. The use of drugs is important but will need the GP and referral to a CAMH service or a paediatrician. ADHD does respond to medication if a careful diagnosis is made, but family work and individual sessions alongside are important. Depression, anxiety, panic attack, and obsessive–compulsive disorder may all respond to medication. This can often be a way to help the young person settle, so that he/she can manage to use a psychological therapy.

Art therapy, drama therapy, and music therapy can be very helpful with some young people. They may be reluctant to talk directly to a professional and feel too old to play. The activity becomes a very useful means for them to communicate what they have problems putting into words.

Difficulties in school with reading, writing, or mathematics may need help from an educational psychologist. Educational therapists are particularly good at helping young people who have problems learning but who cannot express directly what is troubling them. If the problems are more to do with a delay in speech and reading, then speech and language therapists can make a real contribution. If the young person is being bullied, then the school needs to be alerted; in the first instance, some cognitive behavioural therapy to help the young person behave and react differently fast can be helpful.

If the young person is persistently or repeatedly troubled, then help and advice from the local CAMH service is important to clarify the problem. There may be early signs of a more serious mental health problem or there may be unrecognized abuse or drug and alcohol problems.

Anorexia and bulimia need specialist management. Many services now have staff from a range of ethnic minorities and access to interpreters, so they can work with all sections of the population. Foster parents with traumatized young people or refugee young people can find specific services through the Looked After Children teams in social services or the British Association of Fostering & Adoption (BAFA); there are also a number of networks of support for foster-parents.

* * *

Closing reflection

Young people from 10 to 14 years of age are a fascinating mixture of the small child, the academic, the idealist, the depressive, and the experimenter. Turmoil in adolescents is normal, but if this is of excessive intensity and duration, then they need help. They may reject it, and those around them may see the situation as normal, so that problems can become entrenched long before services are accessed.

However, young adolescents respond well to interventions, and hopefulness and enthusiasm are there to be encouraged. Psychoanalytic psychotherapy can work well if the young person can engage with it and if parents and carers support it; family therapy and the other psychological therapies are also effective. The most important factor is what is acceptable to the young person and the family.

useful resources

Organizations

Barnardo's
www.barnardos.org.uk
Head office: 020 8550 8822

Brandon Centre
www.brandon-centre.org.uk

NCH, The Children's Charity
www.nch.org.uk
Head office: 020 7704 7000

NSPCC
www.nspcc.org.uk
Helpline: 0808 800 5000
Asian Helpline: 0800 096 7719

YoungMinds
www.youngminds.org.uk
Head office: 020 7336 8445
Helpline: 0345 626376
Parents Information Service: 0800 018 2138

Publications

Leaflets on mental health, for parents and young people, are available from the Royal College of Psychiatrists:

www.rcpsych.ac.uk/mentalhealthinformation.aspx

and from YoungMinds:

www.youngminds.org.uk/publications

Asperger's Syndrome: A Guide for Parents and Professionals, by T. Attwood. London/Philadelphia: Jessica Kingsley, 1998.

The Many Faces of Asperger's Syndrome, edited by M. Rhode & T. Klauber. Tavistock Clinic Series. London: Karnac, 2004.

Drug-Related Early Intervention: Developing Services for Young People and Families, by the Standing Conference on Drug Abuse. London: SCODA, 1997 (The Good Practice Unit: info@scoda.demon.co.uk).

In a Different World. Parental Drug and Alcohol Use: A Consultation into Its Effects on Children and Families in Liverpool, by the Liverpool Drug and Alcohol Action Team. Liverpool: Liverpool Health Authority, 2001.

Working with Families with Alcohol, Drug and Mental Health Problems, by P. Kearney, E. Levin, & G. Rosen. Report No. 02. London: Social Care Institute for Excellence (SCIE), 2003.

Partners Becoming Parents, edited by C. Clulow. London: Sheldon Press, 1996.

Gillick v West Norfolk & Wisbech Area Health Authority and another. [1985] 3 AU ER 402, [1985] 3AU ER 424b.

Practical Child Psychiatry, by B. Lask, S. Taylor, & K. Nunn. London: BMJ Books, 2003.

Assessment in Child Psychotherapy, edited by M. Rustin & E. Quagliata. Tavistock Clinic Series. London: Duckworth, 2000.

references

Clulow, C. (Ed.) (1996). *Partners Becoming Parents*. London: Sheldon Press.

Gosling, R. (1975). Foreword. In: S. Meyerson (Ed.), *Adolescence and Breakdown*. London: Allen & Unwin.

Long, J., & Trowell, J. (2001). Individual brief therapy with sexually abused girls. *Psychoanalytic Psychotherapy, 15*: 39–59.

Perry, B. D., Pollard, R. A., Blakely, T. L., Baker, W. L., & Vigilante, D. (1995). Childhood trauma, the neurobiology of adaptation and "use-dependent" development of the brain: How "states" become "traits". *Infant Mental Health Journal, 16*: 271–291.

Schore, A. (2001). The effect of early relational trauma on right brain development affect regulation, and infant mental health. *Infant Mental Health Journal, 22*: 201–269.

Trowell, J., Joffe, I., et al. (2007). Childhood depression: A place for psychotherapy. *European Child & Adolescent Psychiatry, 16*: 157–167.

Tsiantis, J. (Ed.). *Work with Parents: Psychoanalytic Psychotherapy with Children and Adolescents*. London: Karnac.

Waddell, M. (2006). Narcissism—an adolescent disorder? *Journal of Child Psychotherapy, 32* (1): 21–34.

index